Contents

Peppery Molasses Cookies 8

Frosted Ginger Creams 8

Pfeffernusse 8

Holiday Fruit Cookies 9

Fancy Peppermint Puffs 10

Gumdrop Jewels 10

Mocha Meringues 11

Oatmeal Crispies 11

Grandpa's Famous Caramels 11

Chocolate Chip Cookies 12

Espresso Bean Cookies 12

Buttery Ricotta Cookies 13

Mom's Gingersnaps 13

4-Spice Crackles 14

Southern Cream Cookies 14

Raisin-Topped Drop Cookies 15

Old-Time Mincemeat Cookies 15

Connie's Orange Cookies 16

Eggnog Cookies 16

Lemon Delights 17

New Year's Cookies 18

Peanut Butter Cookies 18

Frosted Cranberry Drops 19

Cherry Snowballs 19

Amaretti Cookies 20

Butterscotch Chippers 20

Maple-Walnut Drops 21

Raspberry Shortbread Thumbprints 21

Coconut-Pineapple Drops 22

Oatmeal-Cherry Toffee Bites 22

Chocolate-Covered Cherry Cookies 22

Lacy Florentine Cookies 23

Banana Drop Cookies...24

Carrot Cookies..24

Cocoa Gobs..25

Sweet Cinna-Ginger Cookies...25

Spicy Molasses Cookies...26

Grandma's Shortbread...26

Brown Sugar Shortbread Cookies...27

Maple Sugar Cookies...27

Cake Mix Cut-Outs..28

Mom's Sour Cream Cookies..28

Granny's Teacakes...29

Pistachio-Lime Cookies..29

Lemon Tea Cookies...29

Snowflake Crunch Mix...30

Snowman Crispy Pops..30

Gingerbread Men..31

Low-Sugar Cut-Outs..31

Grandma's Molasses Cookies...32

Brown Sugar Hot Tea...32

Chocolate Mint Stars...33

Triple-Layer Chocolate Mints..33

Merry Christmas Hot Punch..34

Christmas Butter Cookies...34

Hungarian Pecan Cookies...34

Iced Shortbread Cookies..35

Raisin-Filled Cookies...35

Jolly Cinna-Men...36

Zesty Lemon Cut-Outs...36

Velvety Butter Cookies...37

Christmas Medallions...37

Pecan Crescent Roll-Ups..38

Buttermilk Sugar Cookies...38

Scottish Jam Biscuits...39

Grandma Talluya's Nutmeg Cookies..40

Santa's Spice Cookies 40

Grammie's Mincemeat Tartlets 41

Turtle Pecan Bars 41

Toffee-Walnut Bars 42

Frosted Mocha Brownies 42

Cranberry Crumb Bars 43

Scotch Oatmeal Bars 43

Grandma's Thumb Bars 43

Classic Lemon Bars 44

Butterscotch Cheesecake Bars 44

Sopaipilla Bars 45

Trail Bars 45

Choco-Berry Goodie Bars 45

Cashew-Macadamia Crunch 46

White Hot Chocolate 46

Old-Fashioned Toffee 47

Gumdrop Bars 47

Cookie Sugarplum Pizza 47

Scrumptious Apricot Bars 48

Fruity Popcorn Bars 48

Nanaimo Bars 49

Chocolate Chip Shortbread 49

Ooey-Gooey S'mores Squares 50

Peanut Butter Bars 50

Molasses Squares 51

Date & Walnut Bars 51

Raspberry-Lemon Bars 52

Apple Butter Bars 52

Sugar Brownies 53

Orangey Brownies 53

Caramel Oat Bars 53

Rocky Road Crunch Bars 54

Chocolate Cherry Bars 54

Brownie Mallow Bars 55

Apricot Nut Bars 55

Scandinavian Almond Bars 55

Pumpkin Jingle Bars 56

Chocolate-Caramel Pecan Bars 56

Heavenly Angel Bars 57

Chocolate Thumbprints 57

Grandma's Springerle 58

Pizzelles 58

Date Sandwich Cookies 59

Rugelach Cookies 59

Coconut Yule Cylinders 59

Holly Wreaths 60

Almond Candy Canes 60

Popcorn Balls 61

Date Pinwheels 61

Polish Cookie Balls 62

Almond Cream Spritz 62

Noels 62

Coffee Eggnog 63

Gingerbread Cottage 63

Royal Icing 63

Cinnamon Hard Candy 64

Candy Strawberries 64

Sparkling Sugarplums 64

Oh-So-Easy Cut-Outs 65

Italian Knot Cookies 65

Chocolate-Almond Fingers 66

Almond Sandies 66

Cinnamon-Sugar Pinwheels 67

Pastel Cream Wafers 67

Two-Tone Icebox Cookies 68

Jam Turnovers 68

Viennese Crescents 69

Golden Tassies 69

Caramel-Coffee Tassies 69

Grandma's Butter Fingers 70

Peppermint Biscotti 70

French Madeleines 71

Raspberry Linzer Tarts 71

Cream-Filled Pecan Snaps 72

Pecan Icebox Cookies 72

Chocolate Cherry Delights 73

Devil's Food Cookies 73

Oatmeal Drop Cookies 74

Peanut Butter Pinwheels 74

Corny Crunch Bars 74

Marbled Cheesecake Bars 75

Peanut Butter Snowballs 75

Merry Christmas Cookies 75

Pecan Pie Bars 76

Gingerbread Pinwheels 76

Chewy Cereal Bars 76

Club Cracker Goodie Bars 77

Butter Brickle Cookies 77

Easy Almond Spritz 77

Peanut Butter Meltaways 78

Graham Kringles 78

Angel Meringues 78

Santa Cookies 79

Quick Fruitcake Bites 79

Tropical Truffles 79

Connie's Sandwich Cookies 80

1-2-3 Cookies 80

Old-Time Skillet Cookies 80

Saucepan Cookies 81

Butterscotch Crunchies 81

Graham No-Bake Cookies 81

Ladybug Cookies 82

Peanut Butter Surprise Cookies 82

Creamy Christmas Eggnog 82

Cocoa Mocha Bites 82

Cinnamon Cornmeal Cookies 83

Peanut Butter & Jam Bars 83

Double Chocolate Brownies 84

Buckeye Brownies 84

Italian Chocolate Cookies 85

Layered Mint Chocolate Fudge 85

Chocolate Peppermint Drops 86

Minty Chocolate Cookie 86

Chocolate-Pecan Biscotti 86

Chocolate-Peanut Butter Balls 87

Chocolate-Orange Snowballs 87

Chocolotta Pizza 88

Brownie Pizza Slices 88

Caramel Pecan Turtles 89

Creamy Chocolate Pecans 89

Chocolate Caramels 89

Espresso Bean Bark 90

Tex-Mex Chocolate Snappers 90

Coconut Bon-Bons 91

Cookies & Vanilla Cream Fudge 91

Mocha Pecan Fudge 91

Morgan's Crinkle Cookies 92

Trillionaire Cookies 92

Chocolate Truffle Cookies 92

Chocolate Bit Meringues 93

Peanut Butter-Chocolate Fingers 93

Double Fudgy Cookie Bars 94

North Pole Candy Cane Fudge 94

Cool Mint Chocolate Swirls 95

Cocoa Buttercream Frosting 95

Homemade Hot Cocoa 95

Nutty Butterscotch Crunch 96

Rocky Road Fudge 96

Choco-Nut Dainties...96

Peppery Molasses Cookies

Ingredients

- 3/4 c. butter, softened
- 1 egg
- 1/4 c. molasses
- 3/4 c. sugar
- 2 c. all-purpose flour
- 2 t. baking soda
- 1/2 t. salt
- 1 t. cinnamon
- 1-1/2 t. pepper
- Garnish: Put extra sugar

Directions

1. Mix butter and sugar in a large bowl till it turns fluffy. Gently beat in an egg; Put in molasses. Whisk together flour and rest of the ingredients. Uniformly Put in to butter mixture; mix properly. Prepare into 1-inch balls and roll in sugar. Make sure you arrange them two inches apart on ungreased baking sheets. Bake at three hundred fifty degrees for twelve to fifteen minutes. Remove and place placed on a wire rack to cool. Prepares four to five dozen.

Frosted Ginger Creams

Ingredients

- 1/2 c. margarine, softened
- 1 egg, beaten
- 1 c. sugar
- 1 c. light molasses
- 4 c. all-purpose flour
- 1/2 t. salt
- 2 t. cinnamon
- 2 t. ground ginger
- 2 t. baking soda
- 1 t. ground cloves
- 1 t. nutmeg
- 1 c. hot water
- Garnish: vanilla frosting

Directions

1. Combine all ingredients excluding frosting in a large bowl. Transfer according to teaspoonfuls to greased baking sheets. Bake at four hundred degrees for eight minutes. Frost using vanilla frosting. Prepares eight dozen.

Pfeffernusse

Ingredients

- 1 c. butter, softened
- 2 eggs, beaten
- 1 t. cinnamon
- 1 c. sugar
- 1/2 t. nutmeg
- 1/4 t. ground cloves
- 1/4 t. allspice
- 1/2 c. corn syrup
- 1/2 c. molasses
- 1/4 c. anise seed
- 1/3 c. water
- 1 t. baking soda
- 6-2/3 c. all-purpose flour
- 5 c. powdered sugar
- 1/2 c. warm water

Directions

1. Mix sugar and butter in a large bowl. Put in eggs and spices; mix properly. Take a different bowl and mix corn syrup, molasses, water and baking soda. Add to the butter mixture. Mix in flour; mix properly. Let it cool for at least 1 hour, till it turns stiff. Roll into three by four-inch balls and Make sure to arrange them on greased baking sheets. Bake at three hundred fifty degrees for ten to fifteen minutes. Allow it to cool for a few minutes. Mix powdered sugar and warm water to form a glaze consistency. Transfer cooled cookies into glaze, a few each time; dry on wire racks. Prepares nine to nine and half dozen.

Holiday Fruit Cookies

Ingredients

- 2-1/4 c. all-purpose flour
- 1/2 t. salt
- 1 c. butter, softened
- 1 t. baking soda
- 2-3/4 c. brown sugar, packed
- 3/4 c. sugar
- 1 t. vanilla extract
- 2 c. crispy rice cereal
- 2 eggs, beaten
- 1 c. mixed candied fruit, finely chopped

Directions

1. Combine flour, baking soda and salt; place aside. Beat together butter and sugars in a large bowl; beat till it is properly blended. Put in eggs and vanilla; beat properly. Uniformly put in flour mixture till properly mixed. Mix in cereal and candied fruit. Transfer according to teaspoonfuls to ungreased baking sheets. Bake at three hundred fifty degrees for about ten minutes. Cool for two minutes prior

to removing from baking sheets. Prepares six dozen.

Fancy Peppermint Puffs

Ingredients

- 2 c. all-purpose flour
- 1/2 c. butter, softened
- 1 c. powdered sugar
- 1/4 t. salt
- 1 egg, beaten
- 1/2 t. vanilla extract
- 8 1-oz. sqs. white baking chocolate, chopped
- 1/2 t. peppermint extract
- 1 t. shortening
- 1/2 c. candy canes, crushed

Directions

1. Combine flour and salt; place aside. Mix together butter and sugar in a large bowl till it turns smooth and creamy. Mix in egg till it is properly blended; Put in extracts. Using an electric blender over low speed, beat in flour mixture. Wrap in plastic wrap; Allow to cool for 1 hour. Make dough into 1-inch balls and place on gently greased baking sheets. Bake at three hundred seventy-five degrees for ten to twelve minutes, till they attain a golden hue. Place over wire racks to cool entirely. Melt chocolate and shortening together; sprinkle over cookies. Immerse cookies in crushed candy; place on wax paper till they are well set. Prepares three dozen.

Gumdrop Jewels

Ingredients

- 1 c. shortening
- 1 c. sugar
- 2 eggs, beaten
- 1 c. brown sugar, packed
- 1 t. vanilla extract
- 1/4 t. salt
- 1 t. baking soda
- 2 c. all-purpose flour
- 1 t. baking powder
- 1 c. gumdrops, chopped
- 1 c. chopped nuts
- 2 c. quick-cooking oats, uncooked

Directions

1. Mix shortening, sugars and eggs; beat till it turns smooth. Mix in rest of the ingredients. Transfer by rounded teaspoonfuls onto ungreased baking sheets. Bake at three hundred fifty degrees for ten to twelve minutes. Prepares two and a half to three dozen.

Mocha Meringues

Ingredients

- 1 t. vanilla extract
- 1/4 t. cream of tartar
- 1 t. instant coffee granules
- 3/4 c. sugar
- 3 T. baking cocoa
- 3 egg whites, at room temperature
- 1/2 c. mini semi-sweet chocolate chips

Directions

1. Mix together vanilla and coffee granules; place aside. Using an electric blender over medium speed, beat together egg whites and cream of tartar till they start to Make froth. Increase speed to medium-high; Put in sugar, one tablespoon each time, and beat till they start to Make firm peaks, about five minutes. Drizzle gently cocoa over egg white mixture. Fold in cocoa using a wooden spoon till they are properly blended. Mix in vanilla mixture and chocolate chips. Transfer by heaping tablespoonfuls onto parchment paper-lined baking sheets. Bake at two hundred fifty degrees for 1 hour without opening the oven door. Time to turn off the oven and tilt door open; leave cookies in the oven for thirty minutes. Take off of the oven; carefully lift cookies up using a thin metal spatula. Prepares three dozen.

Oatmeal Crispies

Ingredients

- 1 c. shortening
- 2 eggs, beaten
- 1 t. vanilla extract
- 1 c. brown sugar, packed
- 1 c. sugar
- 1-1/2 c. all-purpose flour
- 1 t. baking soda
- 1 t. salt
- 2 c. long-cooking oats, uncooked
- Optional: twelve-oz. pkg. semi-sweet chocolate or butterscotch chips, 3/4 c.chopped nuts

Directions

1. Mix together shortening, eggs, vanilla and sugars; mix properly. Take a different bowl and mix flour, baking soda and salt; Put in to shortening mixture. Mix in oats and optional ingredients, if using. Transfer according to teaspoonfuls to greased baking sheets. Bake at three hundred fifty degrees for eight to ten minutes. Prepares five dozen.

Grandpa's Famous Caramels

Ingredients

- 1 c. butter
- 2 c. light corn syrup
- 2 c. sugar
- 2 fourteen-oz. cans sweetened condensed milk, divided
- 1/2 c. all-purpose flour
- 1 t. vanilla extract
- 1-1/2 c. chopped nuts

Directions

1. Melt butter in a heavy saucepan over medium flame. Put in corn syrup and sugar; boil for five minutes, stirring continually. Put in one-one half cans condensed milk. Mix flour with rest of the condensed milk; Put in saucepan. Boil, stirring repetitively, till the point mixture turns dark and reaches firm-ball stage, or two hundred forty four to two hundred forty nine degrees on a candy thermometer. Take off of flame; mix in vanilla and nuts. Pour into a greased 13 inch x 9 inch baking pan and cool entirely. Cut into 1-inch squares; wrap in wax paper. Prepares nine and half to ten dozen pieces.

Chocolate Chip Cookies

Ingredients

- 1/2 c. shortening
- 6 T. sugar
- 6 T. brown sugar, packed
- 1 egg, beaten
- 1/2 t. vanilla extract
- 1-1/8 c. all-purpose flour
- 1/2 t. baking soda
- 1/2 t. salt
- 1 c. semi-sweet chocolate chips

Directions

1. Mix together shortening and sugars; Mix in egg and vanilla. Put in flour, baking soda and salt; mix properly. Mix in chocolate chips. Transfer according to teaspoonfuls to ungreased baking sheets. Bake at three hundred seventy five degrees for ten to twelve minutes, till they attain a golden hue. Prepares about 4 dozen.

Espresso Bean Cookies

Ingredients

- 1/2 c. butter, softened
- 1/2 c. shortening
- 1/4 c. sugar
- 3/4 c. brown sugar, packed

- 2 eggs, beaten
- 1 t. vanilla extract
- 2-1/4 c. all-purpose flour
- 1 t. baking soda
- 1 t. salt
- 1/2 t. cinnamon
- 1 c. chopped almonds, toasted
- 1 c. chocolate-covered coffee beans
- 4 1.4-oz. toffee candy bars, chopped

Directions

1. Using an electric blender over medium speed, beat together butter and shortening till it turns creamy. Uniformly add in sugars, beating properly. Put in eggs and vanilla; mix properly. Mix flour, baking soda, salt and cinnamon. Put in to butter mixture, beating properly. Mix in almonds, coffee beans and chopped candy. Cover and chill dough till it turns stiff. Transfer by heaping teaspoonfuls onto ungreased baking sheets. Bake at three hundred fifty degrees for ten to eleven minutes, until golden. Make use of baking sheets for cooling for 1 minute. Remove to wire racks; cool entirely. Prepares for dozen.

Buttery Ricotta Cookies

Ingredients

- 1/2 c. butter, softened
- 1/4 c. ricotta cheese
- 1 t. vanilla extract
- 1 c. sugar
- 1 egg, beaten
- 2 c. all-purpose flour
- 1/2 t. baking soda
- 1/2 t. salt

Directions

1. Mix together butter and ricotta cheese till it turns creamy. Put in vanilla; mix properly. Uniformly Put in sugar; Mix in egg. Mix in rest of the ingredients. Roll into 1-inch balls and flatten gently on greased baking sheet. Bake at three hundred fifty degrees for ten minutes, or just till the edges attain a golden hue. Place over a wire rack to cool. Prepares twenty.

Mom's Gingersnaps

Ingredients

- 3/4 c. shortening
- 1 c. sugar
- 1/4 c. molasses
- 1 egg, beaten
- 2 c. all-purpose flour

- 2 t. baking soda
- 1/4 t. salt
- 1 t. ground ginger
- 1 t. ground cloves
- 1 t. cinnamon
- Garnish: Put initional sugar

Directions

1. Mix together shortening and sugar. Put in molasses and egg; beat properly. Put in rest of the ingredients excluding garnish; mix properly. Make teaspoonfuls of dough into balls; roll in sugar. Make sure to place them two inches from each other on greased or parchment paper-lined baking sheets. Bake at three hundred fifty degrees for twelve to fifteen minutes. Place over a wire rack to let the cool. Keep in mind to store only in an airtight container for chewy cookies or loosely covered for crisp cookies. Prepares four dozen.

4-Spice Crackles

Ingredients

- 2-1/2 c. all-purpose flour
- 1/2 t. baking soda
- 1/4 t. salt
- 1 t. baking powder
- 1-1/2 t. ground ginger
- 1 t. ground cloves
- 1 t. nutmeg
- 1/2 c. butter, softened
- 1 c. brown sugar, packed
- 1/2 c. shortening
- 1 t. cinnamon
- 1/4 c. molasses
- 1 egg, beaten
- 2/3 c. sugar

Directions

1. Mix flour, baking powder, baking soda, salt and spices; place aside. Take a different bowl and Combine butter, brown sugar and shortening; Mix in molasses and egg. Uniformly Put in flour mixture till it is properly blended. Cover and chill at least 1-1/2 hours. Prepare into 1-inch balls; roll each ball in sugar. Make sure to place them two inches from each other on gently greased baking sheets; flatten gently. Bake at three hundred fifty degrees for nine to twelve minutes, until crackled and centers are soft. Place over a wire rack to let the cool. Prepares two dozen.

Southern Cream Cookies

Ingredients

- 1 c. shortening

- 2 c. sugar
- 3 eggs, beaten
- 1 t. vanilla extract
- 1 c. sour cream
- 5 c. all-purpose flour
- 3/4 t. baking soda
- 1/2 to 1 t. salt
- 1 c. mini semi-sweet chocolate chips

Directions

1. Mix together shortening and sugar; Gently beat in an egg and vanilla. Mix in sour cream and place aside. Whisk flour, baking soda and salt in a different bowl. Put in to shortening mixture; Stir properly. Put in chocolate chips. Transfer according to teaspoonfuls to ungreased baking sheets. Bake at three hundred fifty degrees for fifteen minutes. Prepares about four dozen.

Raisin-Topped Drop Cookies

Ingredients

- 1 c. shortening
- 2 eggs
- 1 t. vanilla extract
- 2 c. brown sugar, packed
- 4 c. all-purpose flour
- 1 t. baking soda
- 5 T. milk

Directions

1. Mix together shortening and brown sugar; Put in eggs, one each time. Mix in vanilla. Take a different bowl and Combine flour and baking soda. Put in alternately with milk to shortening mixture; Transfer by tablespoonfuls onto greased baking sheets. Using a spoon, spread batter to about two inches in diameter. Top with Raisin Topping. Bake at three hundred seventy five degrees for ten minutes. Cool prior to removing from baking sheets. Prepares about three dozen.

Raisin Topping:

- fifteen-oz. pkg. raisins
- 2 T. all-purpose flour
- 1 t. lemon juice
- 1/2 c. sugar

Cover raisins with water in a saucepan. Simmer over medium flame for ten minutes. Combine sugar and flour; Mix in to raisins. Take off of flame when thickened. Cool; mix in lemon juice.

Old-Time Mincemeat Cookies

Ingredients

- 1 c. shortening
- 1 egg, beaten
- 2 c. mincemeat pie filling
- 1-1/2 c. brown sugar, packed
- 3-1/4 c. all-purpose flour
- 1-1/2 t. baking soda
- 1/4 t. salt

Directions

1. Mix together shortening and brown sugar. Put in egg and mincemeat; mix properly. Take a different bowl and Combine flour, baking soda and salt; Mix in to mincemeat mixture. Transfer by rounded teaspoonfuls onto ungreased baking sheets, two inches apart. Bake at three hundred seventy five degrees for eight to ten minutes, until golden. Prepares about six dozen.

Connie's Orange Cookies

Ingredients

- 2/3 c. shortening
- 1 egg, beaten
- 1/2 c. orange juice
- 3/4 c. sugar
- 2 c. all-purpose flour
- 1/2 t. baking powder
- 1/2 t. baking soda
- 1/2 t. salt

Directions

1. Combine shortening, sugar and egg till it is properly blended; Mix in orange juice. Take a different bowl and Mix rest of the ingredients. Uniformly Put in to shortening mixture. Transfer according to teaspoonfuls to ungreased baking sheets. Bake at four hundred degrees for eight to ten minutes. Cool and Frost using Orange Frosting. Prepares three to four dozen.

Orange Frosting:

- 2 T. butter, softened
- 1-1/2 c. powdered sugar
- 1-1/2 to 2 T. orange juice

Mixall ingredients; beat till it turns smooth.

Eggnog Cookies

Ingredients

- 1 c. butter, softened
- 1 c. eggnog
- 1 egg, beaten

* 3-1/2 to 4 c. all-purpose flour
* 1 t. baking powder
* 1 c. sugar
* 1 t. baking soda
* 1/2 t. salt
* Optional: 1/2 t. nutmeg

Directions

1. Combine butter, sugar, eggnog and egg. Put in flour, baking powder, baking soda, salt and nutmeg, if desired. Chill for 1 to two hours, until easy to handle. Transfer by tablespoonfuls onto greased baking sheets. Bake at three hundred fifty degrees for about eight minutes; cool. Frost cookies with Eggnog Frosting when cooled. Make sure to refrigerate only. Prepares about five and half dozen

Eggnog Frosting:

* 1-1/2 c. powdered sugar
* 1/4 to 1/2 c. eggnog

Mix powdered sugar and one fourths cup eggnog. Put in extra eggnog as

needed to reach a spreading consistency

Lemon Delights

Ingredients

* 1 c. butter, softened
* 3-oz. pkg. cream cheese, softened
* 1 egg, separated
* 1 c. sugar
* 1 T. lemon juice
* 1/4 t. salt
* 2-1/4 c. all-purpose flour
* 1 t. vanilla extract
* 2 c. pecans, finely chopped

Directions

1. Mix butter, sugar, cream cheese, lemon juice, egg yolk, vanilla and salt. Mix properly using an electric blender over medium speed; beat in flour. Wrap in plastic wrap; Let it cool for at least 1 hour. Prepare into 1-inch balls. In a small bowl, beat egg white gently. Immerse balls into egg white; roll in pecans. Make sure to place them two inches from each other on ungreased baking sheets. Press thumb deep down into center of each cookie. Spoon Lemon Cheese Filling into indents. Bake at three hundred seventy five degrees for ten minutes, or until filling is properly in place. Cool gently; take off and place over a wire rack. Make sure to refrigerate only in an airtight container. Prepares six dozen.

Lemon Cheese Filling:

* 3-oz. pkg. cream cheese, softened

- 1 drop yellow food coloring
- 1/4 c. sugar
- 1 egg yolk
- 1 T. lemon juice

Beat together all ingredients till it turns smooth.

New Year's Cookies

Ingredients

- 1 c. milk
- 1/4 c. butter, softened
- 1/3 c. sugar
- 2 T. active dry yeast
- 1-1/2 c. raisins
- 1 egg, beaten
- 1 t. lemon juice
- 1/4 t. nutmeg
- 2 t. lemon zest
- 3-1/2 c. all-purpose flour
- oil for deep frying
- Garnish: powdered sugar

Directions

1. Flame milk till the point it is optimally warm, about one hundred ten to one hundred fifteen degrees; cool to lukewarm. Put in yeast; stir to dissolve. Mix in rest of the ingredients excluding oil and powdered sugar. Knead till it turns smooth and elastic. Cover; allow to rise till doubles in bulk. Drop into hot oil according to tablespoons; fry until golden, about two to five minutes. Drain on paper towels and roll in powdered sugar. Prepares two and half dozen.

Peanut Butter Cookies

Ingredients

- 1 c. shortening
- 1 c. sugar
- 1 c. brown sugar, packed
- 2 eggs, beaten
- 1 c. creamy peanut butter
- 3 c. all-purpose flour
- 2 t. baking soda
- 1 t. vanilla extract

Directions

1. Combine shortening and sugars till they turn fluffy and light. Put in eggs and peanut butter, mixing well; place aside. Mix flour and baking soda; Uniformly Put in to peanut butter mixture. Mix in vanilla; mix properly. Prepare into 1-inch balls; place on ungreased baking sheets. Flatten using a

floured fork in a criss-cross pattern. Bake at three hundred fifty degrees for twelve to fifteen minutes.
Prepares about five dozen.

Frosted Cranberry Drops

Ingredients

- 1/2 c. butter, softened
- 3/4 c. brown sugar, packed
- 1/4 c. milk
- 1 egg, beaten
- 1 c. sugar
- 2 T. orange juice
- 1 t. baking powder
- 1/4 t. baking soda
- 3 c. all-purpose flour
- 1/2 t. salt
- 2-1/2 c. cranberries, chopped
- 1 c. chopped walnuts

Directions

1. Mix together butter and sugars in a large bowl. Put in milk, egg and orange juice; mix properly. Take a different bowl and Mix flour, baking powder, baking soda and salt; Put in to butter mixture, mixing well. Mix in berries and nuts. Transfer by tablespoonfuls onto greased baking sheets. Bake at three hundred fifty degrees for twelve to fifteen minutes, until golden. Place placed on a wire rack to cool. Spread cookies with Powdered Sugar Frosting. Prepares about two and half dozen.

Powdered Sugar Frostin g :

- 1/3 c. butter
- 2 c. powdered sugar
- 1-1/2 t. vanilla extract
- 2 T. hot water

Melt butter in a saucepan over low flame until golden, about five minutes. Cool for two minutes; Take off of flame. Put in powdered sugar and vanilla. Beat in hot water, one tablespoon each time, to desired consistency

Cherry Snowballs

Ingredients

- 1 c. butter, softened
- 1 T. water
- 1 t. vanilla extract
- 2-1/2 c. powdered sugar, divided
- 2 c. all-purpose flour
- 1/2 t. salt
- 36 maraschino cherries, patted dry

- 1 c. quick-cooking oats, uncooked
- 1/4 c. milk
- 2 c. sweetened flaked coconut

Directions

1. Mix butter, half cup powdered sugar, water and vanilla; place aside. Take a different bowl and Combine flour, oats and salt; Uniformly Put in to butter mixture. Shape 1 tablespoon dough around each cherry, making a ball. Make sure to place them two inches from each other on ungreased baking sheets. Bake at three hundred fifty degrees for eighteen to twenty minutes, until golden. Place placed on a wire rack to cool. Mix rest of the powdered sugar and enough milk to form a smooth frosting consistency. Immerse cookies in frosting; roll in coconut. Prepares three dozen.

Amaretti Cookies

Ingredients

- 1-1/4 c. whole blanched almonds
- 2 egg whites, at room temperature
- 1/4 t. cream of tartar
- 3/4 c. sugar, divided
- 1/4 t. almond extract
- 1/4 c. slivered almonds

Directions

1. Grind almonds and one fourths cup sugar in a food processor till they are entirely ground; place aside. Using an electric blender over medium speed, beat egg whites, cream of tartar and almond extract until soft peaks form. Uniformly Put in rest of the sugar, one tablespoon each time, beating over high until very stiff peaks appear and sugar is nearly dissolved. Fold in ground almonds. Transfer by rounded teaspoonfuls two inches apart on parchment paper-lined baking sheets. Top each cookie with quite a few slivered almonds. Bake at three hundred degrees for twelve to fifteen minutes, until cookies are gently golden. Turn off oven; let cookies stand in oven with door closed for thirty minutes. Take off the cookies from paper. Keep in mind to store only in an airtight container for up to one week. Prepares about three and half dozen.

Butterscotch Chippers

Ingredients

- 1 c. butter, softened
- 1 c. sugar
- 2 eggs, beaten
- 1 c. brown sugar, packed
- 2-1/2 c. all-purpose flour
- 1 t. baking soda
- 1-1/3 c. butterscotch chips
- 2 c. potato chips, crushed

Directions

1. Combine butter and sugars in a large bowl. Gently beat flour, eggs and baking soda; mix properly. Fold in potato chips and butterscotch chips. Transfer by rounded teaspoonfuls onto gently greased baking sheets. Bake at three hundred fifty degrees for eight to ten minutes. Prepares two dozen.

Maple-Walnut Drops

Ingredients

- 2-1/4 c. all-purpose flour
- 1 t. salt
- 1 c. butter, softened
- 3/4 c. sugar
- 1 t. baking soda
- 1-1/2 t. maple flavoring
- 3/4 c. brown sugar, packed
- 2 eggs, beaten
- 1-1/2 c. chopped walnuts

Directions

1. Mix flour, baking soda and salt in a small bowl; place aside. Take a different bowl and Mix butter, sugars and flavoring till it turns creamy; Gently beat in eggs. Uniformly Mix in flour mixture; mix in walnuts. Transfer by rounded tablespoonfuls one and half inches apart onto ungreased baking sheets. Bake at three hundred seventy five degrees for nine to eleven minutes. Prepares about four dozen.

Raspberry Shortbread Thumbprints

Ingredients

- 1 c. butter, softened
- 2 t. almond extract, divided
- 2 c. all-purpose flour
- 2/3 c. sugar
- 1/2 c. raspberry jam
- 1 c. powdered sugar
- 2 to 3 t. water

Directions

1. Mix butter, sugar and half teaspoon extract. Beat Using an electric blender over medium speed till it turns creamy, two to three minutes. Lower the speed to low. Put in flour; beat till properly mixed. Cover and chill dough for at least 1 hour. Prepare into 1-inch balls. Make sure to place them two inches from each other on ungreased baking sheets. Using thumb, indent the center of each cookie. Fill each indentation with one fourths teaspoon jam. Bake at three hundred fifty degrees for fourteen to sixteen minutes, till the edges attain a golden hue. Allow to stand for 1 minute; Take off of baking sheets and cool entirely. Whisk together powdered sugar, water and rest of the extract till it turns smooth. Sprinkle over cooled cookies. Prepares four dozen.

Coconut-Pineapple Drops

Ingredients

- 3-1/4 c. all-purpose flour
- 1 t. baking soda
- 1/2 t. salt
- 2 t. baking powder
- 1 c. shortening
- 3 eggs, beaten
- 1-1/2 c. sugar
- 1 c. sweetened flaked coconut
- 1 c. crushed pineapple

Directions

1. Combine all ingredients till it is properly blended. Transfer according to teaspoonfuls to greased baking sheets. Bake at three hundred fifty degrees for ten to twelve minutes. Prepares two dozen.

Oatmeal-Cherry Toffee Bites

Ingredients

- 1 c. butter, softened
- 1 c. brown sugar, packed
- 1/2 c. sugar
- 2 eggs
- 1 t. vanilla extract
- 1-1/2 c. all-purpose flour
- 1 t. baking soda
- 1 t. cinnamon
- 3 c. long-cooking oats, uncooked
- 1 c. dried cherries
- 1 c. toffee baking bits

Directions

1. Combine butter and sugars. Gently beat in eggs, one each time; Mix in vanilla and place aside. Take a different bowl and Mix flour, baking soda and cinnamon; Mix in to butter mixture. Mix in oats, cherries and toffee bits. Transfer by rounded teaspoonfuls onto gently greased baking sheets. Bake at three hundred fifty degrees for eight to ten minutes. Cool cookies on baking sheets for five minutes; take off and place over a wire rack. Prepares four dozen.

Chocolate-Covered Cherry Cookies

Ingredients

- 1-1/2 c. all-purpose flour
- 1/4 t. baking powder

- 1/4 t. baking soda
- 1/2 c. baking cocoa
- 1/4 t. salt
- 1/2 c. butter, softened
- 1 c. sugar
- 1 egg, beaten
- 1-1/2 t. vanilla extract
- 48 maraschino cherries, patted dry

Directions

1. Mix together first five ingredients; place aside. Take a different bowl and Mix together butter and sugar till it turns fluffy; Gently beat in an egg and vanilla. Uniformly Put in flour mixture to butter mixture; mix properly. Prepare into 1-inch balls; place on ungreased baking sheets. With a little force place a cherry halfway into each ball; spoon one teaspoon Chocolate Frosting over each cherry. Bake at three hundred fifty degrees for ten to twelve minutes. Place placed on a wire rack to cool. Prepares four dozen.

Chocolate Frostin g :

- 6-oz. pkg. semi-sweet chocolate chips
- 1/2 c. sweetened condensed milk
- 1 to 4 t. maraschino cherry juice

Mix chocolate chips and condensed milk in a saucepan; melt over low flame, stirring continually. Take off of flame; Mix in cherry juice by teaspoonfuls till it turns smooth.

Lacy Florentine Cookies

Ingredients

- 3/4 c. quick-cooking oats, uncooked
- 3/4 c. sugar
- 3/4 c. all-purpose flour
- 1/2 t. baking soda
- 1/2 t. salt
- 1-1/2 c. sliced almonds
- ten T. butter, melted
- 1 t. cinnamon
- 1/4 c. half-and-half
- 1/4 c. light corn syrup
- 1 t. vanilla extract
- 4 1-oz. sqs. semi-sweet baking chocolate, melted

Directions

1. Whisk together oats, flour, baking soda, sugar, salt and cinnamon; Put in almonds. Mix in butter, half-and-half, corn syrup and vanilla till properly combined. Transfer by heaping teaspoonfuls three inches apart onto aluminium foil-lined, greased baking sheets, six cookies per sheet. Bake at three hundred fifty degrees on center rack, one sheet each time, till the edges attain a golden hue, seven to

nine minutes. Cool for quite a few minutes; transfer to a wire rack. Sprinkle melted chocolate over cookies. Prepares four dozen.

Banana Drop Cookies

Ingredients

- 2/3 c. shortening
- 1 t. vanilla extract
- 2 eggs, beaten
- 1-3/4 c. sugar, divided
- 1 c. ripe banana, mashed
- 2 t. baking powder
- 1/4 t. salt
- 2-1/4 c. all-purpose flour
- 1 c. chopped nuts
- 1/2 t. cinnamon

Directions

1. Mix shortening, one and half cups sugar and vanilla till they turn fluffy and light. Put in eggs and beat properly; Mix in mashed banana. Mix in flour, baking powder, salt and nuts; mix properly. Chill for thirty minutes to overnight. Transfer according to teaspoonfuls to greased baking sheets. Mix rest of the sugar and cinnamon together; Drizzle gently on unbaked cookies. Bake at four hundred degrees for eight to ten minutes. Prepares three dozen.

Carrot Cookies

Ingredients

- 1/2 c. shortening
- 1 c. brown sugar, packed
- 1/2 c. butter, softened
- 1 c. sugar
- 2 eggs
- 1 c. carrots, peeled and finely shredded
- 1 c. chopped walnuts
- 1 t. vanilla extract
- Optional: 1/2 c. sweetened flaked coconut
- 2-1/2 c. all-purpose flour
- 1 t. baking powder
- 1 t. baking soda
- 1 t. salt

Directions

1. Mix shortening and butter in a large bowl. Put in sugars, mixing well. Gently beat in an egg, one each time; Put in vanilla. Mix in carrots, walnuts and coconut, if desired; place aside. Take a different bowl and Combine rest of the ingredients. Uniformly Put in to shortening mixture till it is

properly blended; Allow to cool for 1 hour. Transfer by tablespoonfuls two inches apart onto greased baking sheets. Bake at three hundred fifty degrees for eight to ten minutes, until golden. Prepares four dozen.

Cocoa Gobs

Ingredients

- 1/2 c. shortening
- 2 eggs, beaten
- 2 c. sugar
- 1 c. buttermilk
- 3/4 c. boiling water
- 1 t. vanilla extract
- 1/2 c. baking cocoa
- 2 t. baking soda
- 4 c. all-purpose flour
- 1/2 t. baking powder
- 1/2 t. salt
- Garnish: powdered sugar

Directions

1. Mix together shortening, sugar and eggs. Put in buttermilk, boiling water and vanilla; place aside. Take a different bowl and combine flour, cocoa, baking soda, baking powder and salt; Uniformly put in to shortening mixture. Transfer by rounded teaspoonfuls onto ungreased baking sheets. Bake at four hundred fifty degrees for five minutes; cool. Assemble cookies in pairs with filling in between; Drizzle gently powdered sugar over tops and bottoms of cookies. Prepares about two dozen.

Filling :

- 1 c. milk5 T. all-purpose flour
- 1/2 c. butter, softened
- 1/2 c. shortening
- 1 c. powdered sugar
- 1 t. vanilla extract
- 1/4 t. salt

Mix milk and flour in a saucepan over medium flame, stirring continually, until thickened. Cool. Mix rest of the ingredients. Stir milk mixture into butter mixture till it attains consistency of whipped icing

Sweet Cinna-Ginger Cookies

Ingredients

- 6 T. shortening
- 1 c. powdered calorie-free sweetener
- 1 egg, beaten
- 6 T. margarine, softened
- 1/4 c. molasses

- 1 t. cinnamon
- 3/4 t. ground ginger
- 2 c. all-purpose flour
- 1/2 t. ground cloves

Directions

1. Mix shortening, margarine, sweetener, egg and molasses. Take a different bowl and mix rest of the ingredients and put in to shortening mixture; Mix thoroughly. Chill till it turns stiff, about two hours. Make according to tablespoons into thirty balls. Make sure to arrange them on ungreased baking sheets; press down gently using a fork to form a criss-cross pattern. Bake at three hundred fifty degrees for ten to twelve minutes; make sure not to overbake. Place over a wire rack to let the cool. Prepares about two and half dozen.

Spicy Molasses Cookies

Ingredients

- 1 c. butter, softened
- 1/2 c. brown sugar, packed
- 1/2 c. sugar
- 1/2 c. molasses
- 2/3 c. light corn syrup
- 1 t. baking soda
- 1 t. salt
- 4-1/2 c. all-purpose flour
- 1 t. ground ginger
- 1 t. ground cloves
- 1 t. cinnamon
- Garnish: frosting

Directions

1. Mix butter and sugars together. Put in molasses and corn syrup; mix properly. mix dry ingredients and Put in to butter mixture; knead till it turns smooth. Chill for quite a few hours, till it turns stiff. On a gently floured surface, roll out to less than one by eight-inch thick. Cut with floured cookie cutters and place on gently greased baking sheets. Bake at three hundred fifty degrees for eight minutes. Place over a wire rack to let the cool; decorate using frosting as desired. Prepares four to five dozen.

Grandma's Shortbread

Ingredients

- 1 c. butter, softened
- 1/2 c. superfine sugar
- 2 c. all-purpose flour
- 2 T. cornstarch

Directions

1. Mix all ingredients in a medium bowl and knead to make a smooth dough. Roll out on a floured surface to one by four-inch thick. Cut out using a cookie or biscuit cutter. Transfer to ungreased baking sheets. Bake at two hundred seventy five degrees for forty five minutes; cool. Frost using Cream Cheese Frosting. Refrigerate till they are well set or prepare to serve. Prepares two and half dozen.

Cream Cheese Frosting :

- 8-oz. pkg. cream cheese, softened
- 2 t. vanilla extract
- sixteen-oz. pkg. powdered sugar
- 1/2 c. butter, softened
- Optional: few drops food coloring

Using an electric blender over medium speed, beat cream cheese and butter together. Put in vanilla and mix properly. Over low speed, Put in powdered sugar until mixed. Beat over high speed for 1 minute. Tint with food coloring, if required.

Brown Sugar Shortbread Cookies

Ingredients

- 1 c. butter, softened
- 1/2 c. brown sugar, packed
- 2-1/4 c. all-purpose flour

Directions

1. Mix together butter and sugar; Uniformly Mix in flour. Turn onto a gently floured surface and knead till it turns smooth. Pat into an 11 inch x 8 inch rectangle about one by three-inch thick; cut into 2" by 1" strips. Make sure to arrange them on ungreased baking sheets one inch apart. Pierce surface using a fork. Bake at three hundred degrees for twenty five minutes, or until beginning to turn golden on bottom. Cool for five minutes; Place over a wire rack to cool entirely. Prepares three and half dozen

Maple Sugar Cookies

Ingredients

- 1 c. butter-flavored shortening
- 2 eggs
- 1/4 c. maple syrup
- 1-1/4 c. sugar
- 1 T. vanilla extract
- 3/4 t. baking powder
- 3 c. all-purpose flour
- 1/2 t. baking soda
- 1/2 t. salt

Directions

1. Mix together shortening and sugar. Put in eggs, one each time, beating properly after each addition.

Beat in syrup and vanilla. Take a different bowl and mix rest of the ingredients; Uniformly Put in to shortening mixture. Cover and refrigerate for two hours, or until easy to handle. On a gently floured surface, roll out to one by eight-inch thick. Cut using a two and a half-inch cookie cutter Immersed in flour. Make sure to arrange them on ungreased baking sheets one inch apart. Bake at three hundred seventy five degrees for eight to ten minutes, until golden. Remove to wire rack; cool. Prepares two dozen.

Cake Mix Cut-Outs

Ingredients

- 18-1/2 oz. pkg. yellow cake mix
- 1 t. vanilla extract
- 1/2 c. butter, softened
- 2 eggs, beaten
- Garnish: frosting

Directions

2. Mix all ingredients excluding frosting; mix till it turns smooth. Roll dough out on a floured surface to one by four-inch thick; cut into desired shapes with cookie cutters. Place on ungreased baking sheets. Bake at three hundred fifty degrees for twelve to fifteen minutes, until tops are gently golden and edges are done. Cool; frost as desired. Prepares about three dozen.

Mom's Sour Cream Cookies

Ingredients

- 1 c. butter, softened
- 1-1/2 c. sugar
- 1 t. baking powder
- 2 eggs, beaten
- 1-1/2 t. vanilla extract
- 1 c. sour cream
- 4-1/2 c. all-purpose flour
- 1 t. salt
- 1/2 t. nutmeg

Directions

1. Mix together butter and baking powder; put in sugar, eggs, sour cream and vanilla. Mix rest of the ingredients; Uniformly put in to butter mixture. Knead on a floured surface. Roll out to one by four-inch thick and cut out with cookie cutters. Transfer to gently greased baking sheets. Bake at three hundred fifty degrees for fifteen to twenty minutes, until golden; cool. Spread cookies with frosting. Prepares about five dozen

Frosting :

- 1 c. powdered sugar
- 1 T. milk
- 1/2 t. vanilla extract

- few drops food coloring

Mix all ingredients together till it turns creamy

Granny's Teacakes

Ingredients

- 2-1/4 c. sugar, divided
- 5 c. all-purpose flour
- 3 eggs, beaten
- 2 T. buttermilk
- 1 t. baking soda
- 1 t. vanilla extract
- 1 c. butter, softened

Directions

1. Combine two cups sugar and rest of the ingredients. Roll out on a floured surface to one by eight-inch thick. Cut with favorite Christmas cookie cutters. Drizzle gently with reserved sugar. Place over lightly greased baking sheets. Bake at four hundred degrees for ten to twelve minutes, until golden. Prepares two dozen.

Pistachio-Lime Cookies

Ingredients

- 1 c. butter, softened
- 1 egg, beaten
- 2 c. all-purpose flour
- 1 c. sugar
- 1 t. lime zest
- 1 c. pistachios, finely chopped

Directions

1. Beat butter and sugar together; Put in egg. Mix in flour and lime zest; Put in pistachios and mix properly. Cover and Allow to cool for 1 hour. Roll dough out on a floured surface to one by four-inch thick; cut with cookie cutters. Place on ungreased baking sheets. Bake at three hundred seventy five degrees for eight to ten minutes, till they attain a golden hue; cool. Pipe Lime Icing around cookies to outline. Prepares about one and a half dozen.

Lime Icing :

- 2 T. butter, softened
- 1 c. powdered sugar
- 1 T. milk
- 1/4 t. lime zest

Beat together all ingredients till it turns smooth.

Lemon Tea Cookies

Ingredients

- 3/4 c. butter, melted
- 1/4 t. lemon extract
- 1-1/4 c. sugar
- 2 eggs, beaten
- 3-1/4 c. all-purpose flour
- 1/2 t. baking soda
- 1/8 t. salt
- Garnish: Put additional sugar

Directions

1. Mix butter, sugar and extract; Gently beat in an egg. Take a different bowl and combine flour, baking soda and salt; Uniformly put in to butter mixture. Roll out onto a gently floured surface, about one by eight-inch thick. Cut using a round or shaped cookie cutter and place on gently greased baking sheets, one inch apart. Drizzle gently with sugar. Bake at three hundred seventy five degrees for ten to twelve minutes, until golden. Prepares four to five dozen.

Snowflake Crunch Mix

Ingredients

- 1/2 c. margarine
- twelve-oz. pkg. semi-sweet chocolate chips
- twelve-oz. pkg. corn & rice cereal
- 1 c. creamy peanut butter
- 3 c. powdered sugar

Directions

1. Melt peanut butter, margarine and chocolate chips together in a saucepan over low flame, stirring continually, till it is properly blended. Take off of flame. Take cereal into a large bowl and pour chocolate mixture over top; mix carefully. Take powdered sugar into a large brown paper bag. Put in cereal mixture; gently shake to uniformly coat. Allow to cool; make sue to stock in airtight containers. Prepares ten to twelve cups.

Snowman Crispy Pops

Ingredients

- 1/2 c. butter
- 12 c. crispy rice cereal
- ten to twelve wooden skewers
- 2 ten-oz. pkgs. marshmallows
- 8 1-oz. sqs. white baking chocolate, chopped
- Garnish: assorted small candies, broken pretzels, fruit leather

Directions

1. Take butter to a large microwave-safe bowl. Microwave over high setting for about one and half minutes, stirring every thirty seconds. Put in marshmallows; microwave over high setting for three minutes, stirring every minute until melted. Mix in cereal. With buttered hands, pat mixture into an

aluminium foil-lined, greased 15 inch x 10 inch jelly-roll pan. Chill for thirty minutes, or till it turns stiff. Cut out circles using three-inch round cookie cutters. For each snowman pop, insert a skewer through three circles; place aside. Microwave chocolate over high setting for one to one and half minutes until melted; stir till it turns smooth. Spoon melted chocolate over pops to coat. Decorate as required using small candies, with broken pretzels for arms and strips of fruit leather for scarves. Place placed on a wire rack till they are well set. Prepares ten to twelve.

Gingerbread Men

Ingredients

- 1 c. butter, softened
- 1 c. molasses
- 1 c. sugar
- 2 T. ground ginger
- Optional: 1/4 c. crystallized ginger, finely chopped
- 1 t. baking soda
- 1 t. salt
- 5 c. all-purpose flour, divided

Directions

1. Mix together butter, sugar and molasses. Mix in ginger and crystallized ginger, if using. In a large bowl, mix baking soda, salt and one cup flour; Put in to butter mixture. Mix in rest of the flour, one fourths cup each time, and knead by hand since it becomes stiff. Knead till it is properly blended. Roll out onto a gently floured surface to about one by four-inch thick. Cut out desired shapes and make sure to arrange them on parchment paper-lined baking sheets. Bake at three hundred fifty degrees for eight to ten minutes. Prepares four to five dozen.

Low-Sugar Cut-Outs

Ingredients

- 1 c. butter, softened
- 2 eggs
- 2 t. vanilla extract
- 1 c. powdered low-calorie sugar Mixfor baking
- 4 c. all-purpose flour
- 1 t. baking powder
- 1/2 t. salt
- Optional: colored sugar

Directions

1. Using an electric blender over medium speed, beat butter till it turns creamy. Uniformly put in sugar blend, beating properly. Put in eggs, one each time, mixing well. Mix in vanilla. Take a different bowl and mix flour, baking powder and salt. Uniformly Put in to butter mixture. Divide dough in half; pat each half into a circle and wrap using plastic wrap. Allow to cool for 1 hour, until somewhat firm. Roll out one by eight-inch thick on a gently floured surface, one-half of dough each time. Cut out with cookie cutters; place on gently greased baking sheets. Drizzle gently with colored sugar, if required. Bake at 3three hundred twenty five degrees for eight to ten minutes, till they attain

a golden hue around edges. Cool gently on baking sheets; remove to wire racks to cool entirely. Prepares two and half dozen.

Grandma's Molasses Cookies

Ingredients

- 2 c. brown sugar, packed
- 1 c. molasses
- 1/2 c. boiling water
- 1 T. baking soda
- 1-1/2 c. margarine, softened
- 1 t. salt
- 1 t. ground ginger
- 1 t. cinnamon
- 1/2 t. nutmeg
- 1/2 t. ground cloves
- 6 c. all-purpose flour

Directions

1. Mix all ingredients in a large bowl; mix until very stiff. Refrigerate for quite a few hours or overnight. Roll out onto a floured surface to one by four-inch thick. Cut out using a three-inch round cookie cutter; place on ungreased baking sheets. Bake at three hundred fifty degrees for eight to ten minutes; cool. Spread cookies with Creamy White Frosting and let dry. Prepares ten to twelve dozen

Creamy White Frosting :

- 1-1/2 c. sugar
- 1 t. vinegar
- 1 c. mini marshmallows
- 1/2 c. water
- 2 pasteurized egg whites

Mixsugar, water and vinegar in a heavy saucepan over medium-high flame; cover and bring to a boil. Uncover; cook until mixture attains the soft-ball stage, or two hundred thirty five to two hundred forty five degrees on a candy thermometer; Take off of flame. Mix in marshmallows until melted. Beat egg whites till they start to makefroth; Uniformly put in marshmallow mixture. Using an electric blender, beat over high speed until semi-stiff peaks form

Brown Sugar Hot Tea

Ingredients

- 6 c. boiling water
- 6 teabags
- 1/2 c. brown sugar, packed
- Optional: milk or cream

Directions

1. Take a teapot and pour boiling water over teabags into it and cover. Steep for five minutes. Take away teabags and discard. Mix in brown sugar; Put in a splash of milk or cream, if required. Prepares six servings.

Chocolate Mint Stars

Ingredients

- 1-1/4 c. all purpose flour
- 1/2 t. salt
- 1/2 c. baking cocoa
- 1 c. butter, softened
- 1 t. vanilla extract
- 1 c. powdered sugar
- 6-oz. pkg. semi-sweet chocolate chips, chopped
- 1/2 c. peppermint candies, finely crushed

Directions

1. Mix flour, cocoa and salt. Take a different bowl and beat together butter and powdered sugar till it turns smooth; mix in vanilla. Uniformly put in flour mixture to butter mixture and mix properly. Divide in half and wrap inside plastic wrap; chill till it turns stiff, forty five minutes to one hour. Roll out one by four-inch thick on a floured surface, one-half each time. Cut out using a three-inch star-shaped cutter. Arrange 1 inch apart on parchment paper-lined baking sheets. Bake at three hundred degrees on center oven rack, one sheet each time, until tops feel stiff, about twenty five minutes. Make use of baking sheets for cooling for ten minutes. Remove to wire racks; cool entirely. Melt chocolate chips in the top of a double boiler over simmering water; stir till it turns smooth. Sprinkle chocolate over cookies; Drizzle gently with crushed candy. Allow to stand until chocolate is in place, at least 1 hour. Keep in mind to store only in an airtight container at room temperature. Prepares two and half dozen.

Triple-Layer Chocolate Mints

Ingredients

- 6 1-oz. sqs. semi-sweet baking chocolate, chopped
- 1 t. peppermint extract
- 6-oz. pkg. white baking chocolate, chopped
- 4 1.55-oz. milk chocolate bars, chopped

Directions

1. Line an 8 inch x 8 inch baking pan using aluminium foil, leaving a 1-inch overhang on sides; place aside. Take semi-sweet chocolate to the top of double boiler over simmering water; mix till melts entirely. Take off of flame; spread in pan. Allow to stand till it turns stiff. If not firm after forty five minutes, refrigerate for ten minutes. Melt white chocolate in clean double boiler; Mix in extract. Spread over semi-sweet chocolate. Gently shake pan to spread uniformly. Allow to stand for forty five minutes, or till they are well set. Melt milk chocolate in clean double boiler; spread over white chocolate. Shake pan to spread uniformly. Allow to stand for forty five minutes, or till they are well set. Using aluminium foil handles, Take off of pan; place on cutting board. Slice into 1-inch squares. Prepares sixty four pieces.

Merry Christmas Hot Punch

Ingredients

- 2 64-oz. bottles tangerine juice
- 2/3 c. powdered calorie-free sweetener
- Four 4-inch cinnamon sticks
- 5 c. apple juice
- 1 t. cinnamon
- Garnish: orange slices, whole cloves

Directions

1. Mix all ingredients excluding garnish in a large stockpot. Heat to boil over medium-high flame; allow to a simmer for ten minutes. Serve warm, garnished using thin slices of orange, studded along whole cloves. Prepares about forty servings of half cup each.

Christmas Butter Cookies

Ingredients

- 3/4 c. butter, softened
- 1 egg, beaten
- 2 T. evaporated milk
- 1 t. vanilla extract
- 3 c. all-purpose flour
- 1 c. sugar
- 1 t. baking powder
- 1/2 t. baking soda
- 1/2 t. salt

Directions

1. Mix together butter, sugar, egg, evaporated milk and vanilla; mix properly. Put in rest of the ingredients. Roll out on a gently floured surface to one by four-inch thick. Cut out with cookie cutters; place on ungreased baking sheets. Bake at three hundred fifty degrees for about ten minutes, just until golden. Prepares three to four dozen.

Hungarian Pecan Cookies

Ingredients

- 2 c. butter, softened
- 4 c. all-purpose flour
- 2 6-oz. pkgs. pecans, finely ground
- sixteen-oz. container cottage cheese
- 1/2 c. sugar
- 1/4 c. water
- Garnish: powdered sugar

Directions

1. Mix butter and cottage cheese till it is properly blended; Put in flour and mix properly. Cover and chill for quite a few hours, or overnight. Mix pecans, sugar and water; chill, covered for thirty minutes. Roll dough out on a gently floured surface to one by eight-inch thick. Cut into two-inch squares. Spoon half teaspoon pecan mixture into center of every square. Fold opposite corners over filling; press to seal. Prudently transfer to ungreased baking sheets. Bake at three hundred seventy five degrees for eight to ten minutes, until golden. Place placed on a wire rack to cool; roll carefully in powdered sugar just prior to serving. Prepares ten dozen.

Iced Shortbread Cookies

Ingredients

- 2/3 c. butter-flavored shortening
- 2 eggs, beaten
- 1 T. milk
- 1-1/4 c. sugar
- 1 t. vanilla extract
- 2 t. baking powder
- 3 c. all-purpose flour
- 1 t. salt

Directions

1. Mix together shortening, sugar, eggs, milk and vanilla till they are properly blended. Uniformly put in flour, baking powder and salt; mix till it turns smooth. Roll out onto a floured surface and cut into required shapes, or cut out using a drinking glass. Transfer cookies to aluminium foil-lined baking sheets. Bake at three hundred seventy five degrees for eight to ten minutes. Cool entirely; spread with Buttercream Frosting. Prepares about three dozen.

Buttercream Frosting :

- sixteen-oz. pkg. powdered sugar
- 1/4 c. milk
- 1/4 t. salt
- 1/3 c. butter, softened
- Optional: assorted colors food coloring

Beat together all ingredients excluding food coloring till it turns smooth. Put in extra milk to reach required consistency. Divide into separate bowls and put in food coloring, if required.

Raisin-Filled Cookies

Ingredients

- 1 c. shortening
- 1 c. brown sugar, packed
- 3 eggs, beaten
- 1 c. sugar
- 4 c. all-purpose flour
- 1 t. baking soda
- 1/2 t. salt

- 1 t. vanilla extract

Directions

1. Combine all ingredients till properly combined. Roll out on a gently floured surface to one by four-inch thick. Cut out using a round cookie cutter. Spread Raisin Filling onto half the cookies. Arrange rest of the cookies over filling; press edges using a fork Immerse in flour to seal. Bake at three hundred fifty degrees for nine to ten minutes. Prepares three dozen.

Raisin Filling :

- 1 c. raisins, finely chopped
- 1/2 c. water
- 1 T. sugar
- 1 T. all-purpose flour

Combine all ingredients in a saucepan over medium flame. Bring to a boil. Take off of flame; cool gently.

Jolly Cinna-Men

Ingredients

- 1 c. margarine, softened
- 3 eggs, beaten
- 2-1/4 c. brown sugar, packed
- 4 c. all-purpose flour
- 1 t. baking soda
- 1 t. cinnamon

Directions

1. Mix together margarine and brown sugar; Put in eggs and beat properly. Put in rest of the ingredients; mix properly and chill overnight. Divide dough in half and roll out, one portion each time, on a floured surface to one by four-inch thick. Keep rest of the dough refrigerated until prepare to roll out. If dough becomes too tender, place inside the freezer for a few minutes. Cut into required shapes. Bake on a greased baking sheets at three hundred fifty degrees for seven to eight minutes. Prepares about one and a half dozen.

Zesty Lemon Cut-Outs

Ingredients

- 2-1/4 c. all-purpose flour
- 1/4 t. allspice
- 1/8 t. nutmeg
- 3/4 t. cinnamon
- 1/8 t. ground cloves
- 1/8 t. salt
- 3-oz. pkg. cream cheese, softened
- 1/2 c. sugar

- 2/3 c. butter, softened
- 3 T. milk
- 1-1/2 t. lemon zest
- Garnish: candy sprinkles

Directions

1. Whisk together flour, spices and salt; place aside. Take a different bowl and using an electric blender over medium speed, beat together butter, cream cheese and sugar till properly combined. Beat in milk and lemon zest. Uniformly put in flour mixture, beating at low speed just till combined properly. Chill, covered, for two to three hours. On a gently floured surface, roll out dough to about one by eight-inch thick. Cut out shapes using cookie cutters; Make sure to arrange them on ungreased baking sheets. Bake at three hundred fifty degrees for eight to ten minutes, till they attain a golden hue on bottom. Place placed on a wire rack to cool. Frost cooled cookies with Meringue Frosting; decorate with candy sprinkles. Prepares about five dozen.

Meringue Frosting:

- 2 c. powdered sugar
- 4 t. meringue powder
- 1/4 t. cream of tartar
- 3 T. warm water

Mix all ingredients in a medium bowl; beat using an electric blender over low speed till combined properly. Increase to medium-high speed for seven to ten minutes, till they start to make stiff peaks. If too stiff, put in a bit more water, half teaspoon each time. Keep covered until ready to serve

Velvety Butter Cookies

Ingredients

- 2 c. butter, softened
- 2 c. sugar
- 2 egg yolks
- 8-oz. pkg. cream cheese, softened
- 1 t. vanilla extract
- 4-1/2 c. all-purpose flour

Directions

1. Mix all ingredients; mix properly. Chill for two hours. Roll out on a gently floured surface to one by four-inch thick. Cut out using cookie cutters. Bake on greased baking sheets at three hundred fifty degrees for ten to twelve minutes. Prepares seven dozen.

Christmas Medallions

Ingredients

- 1 c. butter, softened
- 1 egg, beaten
- 1-1/2 t. almond extract

- 1/2 t. salt
- 2-1/2 c. all-purpose flour
- 2/3 c. sugar
- 2 T. water
- 2 t. pasteurized dried egg whites
- Garnish: colored sanding sugar

Directions

1. Mix butter, sugar, almond extract, egg and salt in a large bowl. Using an electric blender over medium speed, beat till it turns creamy. Mix in flour over low speed till properly mixed. Divide dough in half; wrap in plastic wrap and chill till it turns stiff, one to two hours. Roll out dough, one-half each time, to one by four-inch thick on a floured surface. Cut out using a two-inch round cookie cutter; Make sure to place them two inches from each other onto ungreased baking sheets. Gently with a little force place a mini cookie cutter into center of each cookie; do not cut through dough. Bake at three hundred fifty degrees for ten to eleven minutes, till they attain a golden hue. Allow to stand one minute; Take off of baking sheets and cool entirely. Whisk water and egg whites together in a small bowl. Using a small brush, paint mixture over center design and rim of each cookie. Drizzle gently with sanding sugar; shake off any extras and allow to dry. Prepares three dozen.

Pecan Crescent Roll-Ups

Ingredients

- 1/2 c. chopped pecans
- 1/4 t. cinnamon
- 1/4 c. sugar
- 1 refrigerated pie crust
- 1 T. water

Directions

1. Mix pecans, sugar and cinnamon in a small bowl; place aside. Unfold crust on a gently floured surface; roll out into a twelve-inch circle. Brush crust with water; spread nut mixture over crust. Using a pizza cutter, divide circle into sixteen wedge-shaped slices. Roll up wedges to make crescents, beginning at outer edge of each slice. Place on gently greased baking sheets one inch apart. Bake at three hundred seventy five degrees for twenty to twenty five minutes, until golden. Prepares about sixteen.

Buttermilk Sugar Cookies

Ingredients

- 1 c. butter, softened
- 2 eggs, beaten
- 2 t. vanilla extract
- 2 c. sugar
- 1/2 c. buttermilk
- 4-1/2 to 6 c. all-purpose flour
- 1 t. baking soda
- 2 t. baking powder

- 1/2 t. salt

Directions

1. Mix together butter and sugar till it turns smooth; Put in eggs and vanilla. Mix until very light. Put in buttermilk and mix gently. Take a different bowl and mix four and half cups flour, baking powder, baking soda and salt. Uniformly put in to butter mixture. Put in more flour, just a bit each time, to form a soft dough that holds together. Wrap with plastic wrap; chill till it turns stiff, two hours or more. Divide dough in half; refrigerate one half and roll out rest of the half, onto a gently floured surface to half-inch thick. Cut into required shapes; transfer to ungreased baking sheets. Repeat with rest of the dough. Bake at three hundred fifty degrees for six to eight minutes, till they attain a golden hue. Cool entirely; frost. Prepares five dozen.

Buttercream Frostin g :

- 1 c. butter, softened32-oz. pkg. powdered sugar
- 1 t. vanilla extract
- 1/4 to 1/2 c. milk
- Optional: food coloring

Beat butter with powdered sugar until light. Put in vanilla and one fourths cup milk; beat till it turns fluffy. Put in more milk to reach required consistency. Divide into smaller bowls; color each using a few drops of food coloring, if desired.

Scottish Jam Biscuits

Ingredients

- 1/2 c. butter, softened
- 2 eggs
- 2 c. all-purpose flour
- 1/2 c. sugar
- 1 T. baking powder
- 1 T. allspice
- 1 T. cinnamon
- 1 c. strawberry jam

Directions

1. Using an electric blender over low speed, Mix butter and sugar till it turns smooth. Gently beat in eggs, one at a time, mixing properly after each addition. Take a different bowl and mix flour, baking powder and spices; Mix in to butter mixture to make a very stiff dough. Roll out on a gently floured surface to one by eight to one by four- inch thick. Cut dough using a round cookie cutter. Make sure to place them two inches from each other onto ungreased baking sheets. Bake at three hundred fifty degrees for ten minutes, or until edges start to turn golden. Place over wire racks to cool entirely. Spread jam on the flat side of 1/2 the cookies; top using another cookie to form a sandwich. Spread frosting on top. Prepares about one and a half dozen.

Frostin g :

- 1/2 c. butter, softened

- 1/8 t. salt
- 3 c. powdered sugar
- 1/4 c. milk, or as needed
- 1-1/2 t. vanilla extract

Beat butter and salt together until tender. Uniformly mix in powdered sugar, milk and vanilla till it turns smooth and light.

Grandma Talluya's Nutmeg Cookies

Ingredients

- 1 c. shortening
- 3 eggs, beaten
- 4 c. all-purpose flour
- 2 c. sugar
- 1 t. baking powder
- 1 t. baking soda
- 3 T. nutmeg
- 1/2 c. milk
- 2 T. white vinegar
- Optional: frosting

Directions

1. Mix shortening and sugar together; Put in eggs. Slowly Put in flour, baking powder, baking soda and nutmeg. Take a different bowl and mix milk and vinegar; slowly mix in to dough. Dough as it is will be very sticky. Turn out onto a floured surface, half the dough each time. Roll to one by four-inch thick. Cut out with cookie cutters; place on parchment-paper lined baking sheets. Bake at three hundred fifty degrees for ten minutes. Cool and frost as desired. Prepares three dozen.

Santa's Spice Cookies

Ingredients

- 1 c. shortening
- 1 egg, beaten
- 1 t. vanilla extract
- 1 c. sugar
- 2 c. all-purpose flour
- 1/2 t. cream of tartar
- 1/4 t. salt
- 1/4 t. nutmeg
- 1/2 t. baking soda
- 1/4 t. ground ginger

Directions

1. Mix shortening, sugar, egg and vanilla till it turns creamy; place aside. In a small bowl, Combine flour, salt, cream of tartar, baking soda, nutmeg and ginger. Uniformly put in to shortening mixture. Turn out onto a gently floured surface. Roll out to one by four-inch thick; cut out shapes with

favorite cookie cutters. Transfer to baking sheets that have been sprayed with nonstick vegetable spray. Bake at four hundred degrees for seven to eight minutes. Prepares two to three dozen.

Grammie's Mincemeat Tartlets

Ingredients

- 3/4 c. shortening
- 2 eggs, beaten
- 3-1/2 c. all-purpose flour
- 1 c. sugar
- 1 T. baking powder
- 1/2 t. salt
- 1/2 t. vanilla extract
- 29-oz. jar mincemeat
- 1/3 c. milk
- Garnish: powdered sugar

Directions

1. Mix together shortening and sugar; Put in eggs. Mix flour, baking powder and salt; place aside. In small bowl, Combine milk and vanilla. Put in to shortening mixture alternately with flour mixture. Chill dough. Roll out to one by four-inch thick and cut using a round cookie or scalloped biscuit cutter. Set about 1 tablespoon mincemeat in the center of each; fold over and press edge using a wet fork to seal. Bake at four hundred degrees for ten to fifteen minutes. Drizzle gently with powdered sugar while still warm. Prepares about two and half dozen.

Turtle Pecan Bars

Ingredients

- 1 c. all-purpose flour
- 1/2 c. butter
- fourteen-oz. can sweetened condensed milk
- 1/2 c. brown sugar, packed
- 2 t. vanilla extract
- 2 c. chopped pecans
- 1 c. sweetened flaked coconut
- twenty vanilla caramels, unwrapped
- 2 T. milk
- 1 c. semi-sweet chocolate chips

Directions

1. Mix together flour and brown sugar. Cut in butter using a pastry blender till the mixture starts to resemble very coarse meal. Press mixture into an ungreased 13 inch x 9 inch baking pan. Bake at three hundred fifty degrees for fifteen minutes; Take off of oven. Mix condensed milk and vanilla. Pour uniformly over baked crust; Drizzle gently with pecans and coconut. Bake at three hundred fifty degrees for twenty five to thirty minutes, until filling sets in place. Place pan placed on a wire rack to cool for ten minutes. Mix caramels and milk in a small saucepan over medium-low flame. Cook and stir till the caramels are melted; sprinkle over top. Drizzle gently with chocolate chips.

Cool entirely placed on a wire rack; cut into little bars. Prepares four dozen.

Toffee-Walnut Bars

Ingredients

- 1 c. butter, softened
- 1/2 t. salt
- 3 T. milk
- 1 t. vanilla extract
- 1/2 c. brown sugar, packed
- 1-1/2 c. all-purpose flour
- 1 c. chopped walnuts, divided
- 6 1.55-oz. milk chocolate candy bars

Directions

1. Beat butter using an electric blender on medium-high speed for thirty seconds. Put in brown sugar and salt; Mix till combined properly. Put in milk and vanilla; Mix in as much flour as possible with mixer. Mix in rest of the flour using a wooden spoon; Mix in half the nuts. Spread batter in a greased 13 inch x 9 inch baking pan. Bake at three hundred fifty degrees for twenty to twenty five minutes, till they attain a golden hue around edges. Arrange chocolate bars on top of hot crust. Allow to stand for a few minutes, until chocolate is melted. Spread chocolate uniformly over crust. Drizzle gently with rest of the nuts. Cool in pan placed on a wire rack; slice into bars. Prepares three dozen.

Frosted Mocha Brownies

Ingredients

- 1 c. sugar
- 1/3 c. plus 1/4 c. baking cocoa, divided
- 1 t. instant coffee granules
- 2 eggs, beaten
- 1/2 c. plus 3 T. butter, softened and divided
- 1-1/2 t. vanilla extract, divided
- 2/3 c. all-purpose flour
- 1/4 t. salt
- 1/2 c. chopped walnuts
- 1/2 t. baking powder
- 2 c. powdered sugar, divided
- 2 to 3 T. milk

Directions

1. Mix sugar, half cup butter, one thirds cup baking cocoa and coffee granules in a medium saucepan. Cook and stir over medium flame until butter is melted. Take off of flame; cool for five minutes. Put in eggs and one teaspoon vanilla; mix just till combined properly. Mix in flour, baking powder and salt; Put in nuts. Spread batter in a greased 9 inch x9 inch baking pan. Bake at three hundred fifty degrees for twenty five minutes, or till they are well set. Cool in pan placed on a wire rack. Beat rest of the butter till they turn fluffy and light; Put in rest of the cocoa. Uniformly put in one cup powdered sugar, mixing well. Mix in two tablespoons milk and rest of the vanilla. Uniformly mix in

rest of the powdered sugar and put extra milk as required to form a spreading consistency. Spread over cooled brownies; slice into bars. Prepares one dozen.

Cranberry Crumb Bars

Ingredients

- 1-1/2 c. plus 1/3 c. all-purpose flour, divided
- 1 c. butter, chilled and divided
- 8-oz. pkg. cream cheese, softened
- 1/3 c. powdered sugar
- 14-oz. can sweetened condensed milk
- 1/4 c. lemon juice
- 2 T. cornstarch
- 3 T. brown sugar, packed and divided
- 16-oz. can whole-berry cranberry sauce
- 3/4 c. walnuts, finely chopped

Directions

1. Mix one and half cups flour and powdered sugar; cut in three fourths cup butter until crumbly. Press into a greased 13 inch x 9 inch baking pan. Bake at three hundred fifty degrees for fifteen to twenty minutes, till the edges attain a golden hue. Take off of oven. Beat cream cheese till it turns smooth. Put in condensed milk and lemon juice; mix properly and spread over baked crust. Take a different bowl and mix corn starch and one tablespoon brown sugar. Mix in cranberry sauce till combined properly. Spread over cream cheese layer and place aside. Mix brown sugar and rest of the flour; cut in rest of the butter. Mix in nuts; Drizzle gently over filling. Bake at three hundred twenty five degrees for forty to forty five minutes, until topping is golden. Cool in pan placed on a wire rack. Cover and chill for three hours prior to slicing into bars. Prepares one dozen.

Scotch Oatmeal Bars

Ingredients

- 3/4 c. butter, softened
- 2/3 c. sugar
- 1/2 c. all-purpose flour
- 3 c. long-cooking oats, uncooked
- 2/3 c. semi-sweet chocolate chunks
- 1 t. vanilla extract
- 1/2 t. salt

Directions

1. Mix together all ingredients by hand till it is properly blended. Press into an ungreased 13 inch x 9 inch baking pan. Bake at three hundred fifty degrees for thirty minutes. Cut into bars. Prepares one and a half dozen.

Grandma's Thumb Bars

Ingredients

- 1/2 c. shortening
- 1/2 t. salt
- 1 c. plus 2 T. all-purpose flour
- 1-1/2 c. dark brown sugar, packed and divided
- 1/2 t. baking powder
- 2 eggs, beaten
- 1 t. vanilla extract
- 1-1/2 c. sweetened flaked coconut
- 1 c. chopped walnuts

Directions

1. Mix shortening and half cup brown sugar till it turns smooth. Mix in salt and one cup flour till it is properly blended. Press into a greased 13 inch x 9 inch baking pan. Bake at three hundred twenty five degrees for fifteen minutes, or until golden. Take off of oven; Allow to cool. Take a different bowl and combine rest of the brown sugar, baking powder and rest of the flour till it is properly blended. Mix in eggs and vanilla, beating until thick and foamy. Mix in coconut and nuts; spread over baked crust. Bake at three hundred fifty degrees for thirty five minutes, or until bars are gently golden and puffy. Cool entirely; slice into thirty six tiny bars. Prepares three dozen.

Classic Lemon Bars

Ingredients

- 1 c. butter, softened
- 1/2 c. powdered sugar
- 2-1/4 c. all-purpose flour, divided
- 1/8 t. salt
- 2 c. sugar
- 4 eggs, beaten
- 6 T. lemon juice
- Garnish: Put in extra powdered sugar

Directions

1. Mix butter, two cups flour, powdered sugar and salt; mix properly. Press into an ungreased 13 inch x 9 inch baking pan. Bake at three hundred fifty degrees for fifteen minutes until golden. Mix sugar and rest of the flour in a large bowl; Mix in eggs and lemon juice. Pour onto gently cooled crust. Bake at three hundred fifty degrees for twenty five minutes. Cool; Drizzle gently with powdered sugar. Slice into bars. Prepares fifteen to eighteen.

Butterscotch Cheesecake Bars

Ingredients

- 6-oz. pkg. butterscotch chips
- 2 c. graham cracker crumbs
- 1/3 c. butter
- 1 c. chopped pecans
- 8-oz. pkg. cream cheese, softened

- 14-oz. can sweetened condensed milk
- 1 t. vanilla extract
- 1 egg, beaten

Directions

1. Melt butterscotch chips and butter in a saucepan over medium-low flame; Mix in cracker crumbs and pecans. Press half of mixture into an ungreased 13 inch x 9 inch baking pan. Beat cream cheese in a large bowl till it turns fluffy; Mix in condensed milk. Put in vanilla and egg; mix properly and pour over crumb mixture. Top with rest of the crumb mixture. Bake at three hundred fifty degrees for twenty five to thirty minutes. Chill till it turns stiff; cut into bars. Prepares about one and a half dozen.

Sopaipilla Bars

Ingredients

- 2 8-oz. tubes refrigerated crescent rolls, divided
- 1-1/2 c. sugar, divided
- 1 t. vanilla extract
- 8-oz. pkg. cream cheese, softened
- 1 t. cinnamon
- 1/2 c. butter, melted

Directions

1. Press one tube crescent rolls into an ungreased 13 inch x 9 inch baking pan; place aside. Mix cream cheese, one cup sugar and vanilla in a small bowl. Spread cream cheese mixture in crescent patterns in baking pan. Arrange rest of the crescent rolls over cream cheese layer. In a small bowl, mix rest of the sugar and cinnamon; Drizzle gently over crescents. Sprinkle melted butter over top. Bake at three hundred fifty degrees for twenty five to thirty minutes. Allow to cool to room temperature; slice into bars. Prepares about one and a half dozen.

Trail Bars

Ingredients

- 1 c. creamy peanut butter
- 1 c. honey
- 1 c. semi-sweet chocolate chips
- 4 c. quick-cooking oats, uncooked

Directions

1. Combine peanut butter and honey; Mix in chocolate chips and oats. Press into a gently greased 13 inch x 9 inch baking pan. Cover and refrigerate until prepare to serve; cut into bars. Prepares one and a half dozen.

Choco-Berry Goodie Bars

Ingredients

- 3 c. quick-cooking oats, uncooked

- 2 T. butter, melted
- 1 c. sweetened flaked coconut
- 14-oz. can sweetened condensed milk
- 1 c. sliced almonds
- 1 c. mini semi-sweet chocolate chips
- 1/2 c. sweetened dried cranberries

Directions

1. Mix all ingredients in a large bowl; use hands to mix properly. Press into a greased 13 inch x 9 inch baking pan. Bake at three hundred fifty degrees for twenty to twenty five minutes, till the edges attain a golden hue. Cool for five minutes; slice into squares and cool entirely. Prepares two dozen.

Cashew-Macadamia Crunch

Ingredients

- 12-oz. pkg. milk chocolate chips
- 1/2 c. sugar
- 1/2 c. butter, softened
- 2 T. light corn syrup
- 3/4 c. cashews, coarsely chopped
- 3/4 c. macadamia nuts, coarsely chopped

Directions

1. Line a 9 inch x 9 inch baking pan using aluminium foil outspreading over edges of pan. Drizzle gently chocolate chips in pan; place aside. Mix butter, sugar, corn syrup and nuts in a skillet over low flame, stirring continually. Cook until butter is melted and sugar is dissolved. Increase flame to medium, stirring continually; cook until mixture begins to cling together and attains a golden hue. Pour over chocolate chips in pan, spreading uniformly. Cool; refrigerate till it turns stiff. Take off of pan using aluminium foil edges as a handle; peel off foil. Break into pieces. Prepares about two pounds.

White Hot Chocolate

Ingredients

- 6-oz. pkg. white chocolate chips
- Optional: 1/4 t. cayenne pepper
- 1/2 to 1 t. cinnamon
- 1 egg, beaten
- 3-1/4 c. milk, divided
- Optional: Put initional cinnamon

Directions

1. Place chocolate chips in a metal bowl over a pan of barely simmering water. Mix till it turns smooth. Mix in spices; whisk in egg till it turns smooth. Uniformly whisk in one cup milk till they are properly blended, about two minutes. Mix in rest of the milk; heat till it turns hot but not boiling. Take using ladle into mugs; Drizzle gently with extra cinnamon, if required. Serves four.

Old-Fashioned Toffee

Ingredients

- 1 c. butter
- 1/8 t. salt
- 1 T. light corn syrup
- 1-1/3 c. sugar
- 3 T. water
- twelve-oz. pkg. milk chocolate chips

Directions

1. Melt butter in a large saucepan over medium flame. Put in sugar, salt, corn syrup and water. Cook, stirring occasionally, until a candy thermometer reaches two hundred seventy five degrees. Continue to cook, stirring continually, until candy thermometer reaches three hundred degrees. Spread onto an ungreased baking sheet; cool entirely. Melt 1/2 of chocolate chips; spread over cooled toffee. Cool entirely. Cover using a different baking sheet and turn over. Melt rest of the chocolate chips and spread over other side. Cool entirely. Break into one to two-inch pieces. Prepares about two pounds

Gumdrop Bars

Ingredients

- 1/2 c. butter
- 1/2 t. baking powder
- 1/2 t. salt
- 1-1/2 c. brown sugar, packed
- 2 eggs, beaten
- 1/2 c. chopped nuts
- 1 c. gumdrops, chopped
- 1-1/2 c. all-purpose flour
- 1 t. vanilla extract
- Garnish: powdered sugar

Directions

1. Melt butter in a saucepan; Mix in rest of the ingredients excluding powdered sugar. Spread in a greased and floured 13 inch x 9 inch baking pan. Bake at three hundred fifty degrees for twenty five to thirty minutes, until golden. Drizzle gently with powdered sugar. Cool and slice into bars. Prepares two dozen.

Cookie Sugarplum Pizza

Ingredients

- 2/3 c. butter, softened
- 1/2 t. baking soda
- 1 t. ground ginger
- 3/4 c. sugar
- 1/2 t. cinnamon

- 1 egg, beaten
- 2 T. molasses
- 1-3/4 c. all-purpose flour
- 1-3/4 c. mini gumdrops
- 1/2 c. white chocolate chips
- 1-1/2 t. butter-flavored shortening

Directions

1. In a large bowl, using an electric blender on medium-high speed, beat butter for thirty seconds. Put in sugar, baking soda and spices; beat till combined properly. Gently beat in an egg and molasses; beat in as much flour as possible with mixer. Use a wooden spoon to mix in any rest of the flour. Pat uniformly into a gently greased twelve" round pizza pan. Bake at three hundred fifty degrees for twelve minutes. Drizzle gently gumdrops over baked crust; bake an put extra eight minutes, or till the edges attain a golden hue. Cool entirely in pan placed on a wire rack. In a small saucepan over low flame, melt chocolate chips and shortening; sprinkle over cookie. Allow to stand twenty to thirty minutes, till they are well set; cut into thin wedges. Prepares sixteen servings.

Scrumptious Apricot Bars

Ingredients

- 1 c. all-purpose flour
- 1 t. baking powder
- 1 egg, beaten
- 1 T. milk
- 1/2 c. margarine, softened
- 3/4 c. apricot preserves

Directions

1. Mix flour, baking powder and margarine; Put in egg and milk. Press into a greased 9 inch x 9 inch baking pan; spread with preserves and place aside. Spread Coconut Topping over preserves. Bake at three hundred fifty degrees for twenty five to thirty minutes. Cut into bars. Prepares one dozen.

Coconut Toppin g :

- 1/4 c. margarine, softened
- 1 c. sugar
- 1 egg, beaten
- 1 t. vanilla extract
- 1 c. sweetened flaked coconut

Mix margarine and sugar. Put in egg and vanilla; Mix in coconut.

Fruity Popcorn Bars

Ingredients

- 3-oz. pkg. microwave popcorn, popped
- 3/4 c. sweetened dried cranberries
- 3/4 c. white chocolate chips

- 1/2 c. sweetened flaked coconut
- 1/2 c. slivered almonds, coarsely chopped
- ten-oz. pkg. marshmallows
- 3 T. butter

Directions

1. Line a 13 inch x 9 inch baking pan using aluminium foil; spray gently with non-stick vegetable spray. Toss together popcorn, chocolate chips, cranberries, coconut and almonds in a large bowl; place aside. Melt marshmallows and butter in a saucepan over medium flame; stir till it turns smooth. Pour over popcorn mixture and toss to coat entirely; quickly pour into prepared pan. Lay a sheet of wax paper over top and press down firmly. Chill for thirty minutes, or till it turns stiff. Lift bars from pan, using foil as handles; peel off foil and wax paper. Slice into bars and chill an put extra thirty minutes. Prepares sixteen.

Nanaimo Bars

Ingredients

- 1 c. plus 1 T. butter, softened and divided
- 1-oz. sq. unsweetened baking chocolate, chopped
- 1 t. vanilla extract
- 1 egg, beaten
- 1/4 c. sugar
- 2 c. graham cracker crumbs
- 1/2 c. chopped nuts
- 2 T. instant vanilla pudding mix
- 1 c. sweetened flaked coconut
- 2 c. powdered sugar
- 3 T. milk
- 4 1-oz. sqs. semi-sweet baking chocolate, chopped

Directions

1. Mix half cup butter, sugar and unsweetened chocolate in a double boiler over medium flame. Cook till it is properly blended; Mix in vanilla. Put in egg; cook for five minutes. Take off of flame; Mix in crumbs, nuts and coconut. Press into a greased 13 inch x 9 inch baking pan; chill for fifteen minutes. Beat half cup butter till it turns fluffy; Mix in pudding mix, powdered sugar and milk. Spread over mixture. Melt semi-sweet chocolate and rest of the butter over low flame till it is properly blended. Spread over top; chill prior to cutting into bars. Prepares about three and half dozen

Chocolate Chip Shortbread

Ingredients

- 1 c. butter, softened
- 1-3/4 c. all-purpose flour
- 1/4 c. cornstarch
- 1/3 c. sugar
- 1 c. mini semi-sweet chocolate chips

Directions

1. Mix butter and sugar in a large bowl. Using an electric blender, beat at medium speed till it turns creamy, one to two minutes. Lower the speed to low. Put in flour and cornstarch; beat till properly mixed, one to two minutes. Mix in chips. Press into an ungreased 13 inch x 9 inch baking pan; pierce all over using a fork. Bake at three hundred fifty degrees for thirty five to forty five minutes, just until edges begin to turn golden. In case edges begin getting too dark, cover with aluminium foil. Cool in pan fifteen minutes; slice into bars while still warm. Prepares one and a half dozen.

Ooey-Gooey S'mores Squares

Ingredients

- 2 sleeves graham crackers, crushed and divided
- 1 c. butter, melted and divided
- 8 1.55-oz. milk chocolate candy bars, divided
- 7-oz. jar marshmallow creme, divided
- 1/4 c. sugar, divided
- 1 sleeve chocolate graham crackers, crushed

Directions

1. Mix plain graham cracker crumbs and sugar; Mix in two thirds cup butter. Place aside half of crumb mixture; press the rest into a gently greased 8 inch x 8 inch baking pan. Bake at three hundred twenty five degrees for ten minutes; cool gently. Break chocolate bars in 1/2; spread along marshmallow creme. Arrange half the bars over crust, breaking into smaller pieces to form them fit. Mix chocolate graham cracker crumbs with rest of the butter. Spread mixture over marshmallow creme-covered chocolate bars; press lightly. Arrange rest of the chocolate bars over chocolate graham layer. Spread reserved plain crumb mixture over top; press down lightly. Bake at three hundred twenty five degrees for fifteen to twenty minutes. Cool entirely, about ninety minutes to two hours. Slice into squares. Prepares sixteen to twenty five.

Peanut Butter Bars

Ingredients

- 1/2 c. butter, softened
- 1/2 c. brown sugar, packed
- 1 egg, beaten
- 1/2 c. sugar
- 1/2 c. creamy peanut butter
- 1/2 t. baking soda
- 1/2 t. vanilla extract
- 1/4 t. salt
- 1 c. all-purpose flour
- 1 c. long-cooking oats, uncooked

Directions

1. Mix butter and sugars in a large bowl. Put in egg, peanut butter, baking soda, salt and vanilla; Mix in flour and oats. Spread into a greased 13 inch x 9 inch baking pan. Bake at three hundred fifty

degrees for twenty to twenty five minutes; cool and Frost using Peanut Butter Icing. Cut into bars. Prepares two dozen

Peanut Butter Icin:

- 1/2 c. butter, softened
- 1 c. creamy peanut butter
- 2 c. powdered sugar
- 3 T. milk

Beat butter and peanut butter together till they turns smooth. Uniformly Put in powdered sugar. Beat in milk, one tablespoon each time, as mixture gets thicker. Beat for three minutes, till it turns fluffy.

Molasses Squares

Ingredients

- 1/2 c. molasses
- 1/2 c. brown sugar, packed
- 1 egg, beaten
- 1/2 c. shortening
- 1/2 c. milk
- 2 t. vanilla extract, divided
- 1-1/2 t. baking powder
- 2 c. all-purpose flour
- 1/4 t. baking soda
- 1/2 t. salt
- 1 c. powdered sugar
- 2 to 3 T. milk

Directions

1. Mix first six ingredients in a large bowl; mix properly. Mix together flour, baking powder, baking soda and salt; Uniformly Put in to molasses mixture. Spread into a greased 13 inch x 9 inch baking pan. Bake at three hundred fifty degrees for twenty minutes. Mix powdered sugar, rest of the vanilla and milk; mix properly. Spread over top while still warm. Slice into squares. Prepares two dozen.

Date & Walnut Bars

Ingredients

- sixteen-oz. pkg. chopped dates
- 1 c. water
- 1 t. vanilla extract
- 3/4 c. sugar
- 1 c. chopped walnuts
- 3/4 c. plus 1 T. butter, melted and divided
- 1-1/2 c. all-purpose flour
- 1/2 t. baking powder
- 1-3/4 c. long-cooking oats, uncooked
- 1 t. baking soda

- 1/2 t. salt
- 1 c. brown sugar, packed

Directions

1. Mix dates, sugar and water in a large saucepan over medium flame. Bring to a boil; simmer for five to ten minutes, until thick. Mix in vanilla, walnuts and one tablespoon butter; place aside to cool gently. Mix rest of the ingredients, including butter. Press half of oat mixture into a gently greased 13 inch x 9 inch baking pan; spread date mixture over top. Cover with rest of the half of oat mixture; press gently. Bake at three hundred fifty degrees for twenty five minutes. Cool entirely prior to slicing into squares. Prepares two to two and half dozen.

Raspberry-Lemon Bars

Ingredients

- 3/4 c. plus 2 T. all-purpose flour, divided
- 1/8 t. salt
- 1/4 c. butter
- 2 c. powdered calorie-free sweetener, divided
- 1/2 c. egg substitute
- 1/2 c. half-and-half
- 1/2 c. lemon juice
- 1 T. lemon zest
- 1/4 c. reduced-sugar raspberry preserves

Directions

1. Combine three fourths cup flour, three fourths cup sweetener and salt in a medium bowl. Cut in butter till the mixture turns crumbly. Press dough into a gently greased 8 inch x 8 inch baking pan. Bake at three hundred fifty degrees for fifteen to twenty minutes, until golden. Mix rest of the sweetener and flour in a medium bowl; mix properly. Put in egg substitute and half-and-half; stir till they are properly blended. Slowly Put in lemon juice, stirring continually; Mix in zest. Spread preserves uniformly over warm crust. Gently pour lemon mixture over preserves. Bake at three hundred fifty degrees for twenty to twenty five minutes, till they are well set. Take off of oven; cool entirely. Chill for two hours prior to cutting into bars. Prepares sixteen to twenty.

Apple Butter Bars

Ingredients

- 1-1/2 c. all-purpose flour
- 1 t. salt
- 1-1/2 c. quick-cooking oats, uncooked
- 1 t. baking soda
- 1-1/2 c. sugar
- 1 c. butter, melted
- 1-1/2 c. apple butter
- 1 c. chopped pecans or walnuts

Directions

1. Mix flour, baking soda and salt in a large bowl. Mix in oats and sugar. Put in melted butter; mix properly until crumbly. Press half of mixture into a greased 13 inch x 9 inch baking pan; place aside. Mix apple butter and nuts together: spread over crumb mixture. Drizzle gently with rest of the crumb mixture. Bake at three hundred fifty degrees for fifty to sixty minutes, until golden. Cool entirely; slice into bars. Prepares about two and half dozen.

Sugar Brownies

Ingredients

- 2/3 c. butter, softened
- 4 eggs, beaten
- 2-1/4 c. brown sugar, packed
- 2 c. all-purpose flour
- 2 t. baking powder
- 1 t. salt
- 1 t. vanilla extract
- 6-oz. pkg. semi-sweet chocolate chips

Directions

1. Using an electric blender, beat together butter and brown sugar in a small bowl; Gently beat in eggs. Take a different bowl and combine flour, baking powder, salt and vanilla; stir in butter mixture. Mix in chocolate chips; spoon batter into a greased 13 inch x 9 inch baking pan. Bake at three hundred fifty degrees for thirty five to forty minutes, until a toothpick tests clean. Cut into squares. Prepares about one and a half dozen.

Orangey Brownies

Ingredients

- 1-1/2 c. all-purpose flour
- 3/4 t. salt
- 1-3/4 c. sugar
- 1 c. butter, softened
- 4 eggs, beaten
- 2 t. orange extract
- 2 T. orange zest, divided
- 1 c. powdered sugar
- 2 T. orange juice

Directions

1. Mix together flour, sugar and salt in a large bowl; Put in butter, eggs, extract and one tablespoon zest. Beat mixture till it is properly blended; pour into a greased 13 inch x 9 inch baking pan. Bake at three hundred fifty degrees for thirty minutes, or till they attain a golden hue and center is set. Take off of oven; pierce entire top using a fork. In a small bowl, combine powdered sugar, orange juice and rest of the zest; spread over brownies. Cool entirely; slice into squares. Prepares one dozen.

Caramel Oat Bars

Ingredients

- 32 caramels, unwrapped
- 1 c. long-cooking oats, uncooked
- 5 T. whipping cream
- 1 c. all-purpose flour
- 1/2 t. baking soda
- 1/4 t. salt
- 3/4 c. brown sugar, packed
- 3/4 c. butter, melted
- 1/2 c. semi-sweet chocolate chips
- 1/2 c. chopped walnuts

Directions

1. Mix caramels and cream in a saucepan over low flame, stirring occasionally till it turns smooth; place aside. Combine oats, brown sugar, baking soda, flour and salt in a medium bowl; Mix in melted butter until crumbly. Press half the mixture into a gently greased 13 inch x 9 inch baking pan. Bake at three hundred fifty degrees for eight minutes. Take off of oven; Drizzle gently with chocolate chips and walnuts. Pour caramel mixture over top; Drizzle gently with rest of the oat mixture. Return to oven and bake for an extra twelve minutes, or until top is gently toasted. Slice into bars while still warm. Prepares about two dozen.

Rocky Road Crunch Bars

Ingredients

- 1/3 c. honey
- 4 c. mini marshmallows
- 4 c. granola or oat cluster cereal
- 3 T. butter
- 2 T. creamy or crunchy peanut butter
- 4 1-oz. sqs. semi-sweet baking chocolate, chopped

Directions

1. Mix honey and butter in a microwave-safe bowl; microwave over high setting for one minute. Stir till it is properly blended. Put in mini marshmallows; toss to coat. Microwave over high setting for ninety seconds, or until marshmallows are puffed. Mix in rest of the ingredients. Press into a greased 13 inch x 9 inch baking pan; chill. Cut into bars. Prepares two dozen.

Chocolate Cherry Bars

Ingredients

- 1/2 c. butter, melted
- fourteen-oz. can sweetened condensed milk
- twelve-oz. pkg. milk chocolate chips
- 1-1/2 c. graham cracker crumbs
- ten-oz. jar maraschino cherries, drained and chopped

Directions

1. Spread melted butter uniformly in a 13 inch x 9 inch baking pan. Mix in graham cracker crumbs; press down to make a crust. Pour condensed milk over top; Drizzle gently with chocolate chips and chopped cherries. Bake at three hundred fifty degrees for twenty five minutes. Cool entirely; slice into bars. Prepares about two dozen.

Brownie Mallow Bars

Ingredients

- 21-oz. pkg. fudge brownie mix
- twelve-oz. pkg. semi-sweet chocolate chips
- 1 c. creamy peanut butter
- 7-oz. jar marshmallow creme
- 1 T. butter
- 1 c. crispy rice cereal

Directions

1. Make brownie mix according to box **Directions**; pour into a greased 13 inch x 9 inch baking pan. Bake at three hundred fifty degrees for twenty eight to thirty minutes. Carefully spread marshmallow creme over hot brownies; cool. Mix chocolate chips, peanut butter and butter in a microwave-safe bowl. Microwave over high setting for two to three minutes, stirring every thirty seconds, till it turns smooth. Mix in cereal; mix lightly and spread over brownies. Refrigerate for 1 to two hours till it turns stiff, prior to slicing into bars. Prepares two to two and half dozen.

Apricot Nut Bars

Ingredients

- 1-1/2 c. all-purpose flour
- 1/2 c. plus 1 T. butter, softened and divided
- 1/4 c. shortening
- 3/4 c. powdered sugar
- 1 egg, beaten
- 1/2 c. sugar
- 1/2 c. apricot preserves
- 1/2 t. vanilla extract
- 1 c. sliced almonds

Directions

1. Mix flour, powdered sugar, half cup butter and shortening in a large bowl; beat till it is properly blended. Pat into an ungreased 13 inch x 9 inch baking pan. Bake at three hundred fifty degrees for eighteen to twenty minutes, until golden. In a small bowl, beat egg, sugar, preserves, rest of the butter and vanilla till it turns smooth. Spread over hot crust; Drizzle gently using almonds. Bake at three hundred fifty for fifteen to twenty minutes. Cool and cut into bars. Prepares two and half to three dozen.

Scandinavian Almond Bars

Ingredients

- 1/2 c. butter, softened
- 1 egg, beaten
- 1 c. sugar
- 3/4 t. almond extract, divided
- 1-3/4 c. all-purpose flour
- 2 t. baking powder
- 1/4 t. salt
- 2 to 3 T. milk, divided
- 1/2 c. sliced almonds, chopped
- 1 c. powdered sugar

Directions

1. Mix together butter and sugar in a large bowl; Gently beat in an egg and ½ teaspoon extract. Mix flour, baking powder and salt; Uniformly Put in to butter mixture and mix properly. Divide dough into fourths; Prepare into twelve"x3" rectangles. Place five inches apart on greased baking sheets. Brush with 1 tablespoon milk; Drizzle gently using almonds. Bake at three hundred twenty five degrees for eighteen to twenty minutes, till they are well set and edges are golden. Make use of baking sheets for cooling for five minutes; cut diagonally into 1-inch slices. Remove to wire racks to cool entirely. Mix powdered sugar, rest of the extract and enough of rest of the milk to form a drizzling consistency; sprinkle over bars. Prepares four dozen.

Pumpkin Jingle Bars

Ingredients

- eighteen-1/2 oz. pkg. spice cake mix
- 3/4 c. mayonnaise-type salad dressing
- sixteen-oz. can pumpkin
- 3 eggs, beaten
- sixteen-oz. container vanilla frosting
- Garnish: red and green gumdrops, sliced

Directions

1. Using an electric blender over medium speed, beat together first 4 ingredients in a large bowl till it is properly blended. Pour into a greased 15 inch x 10 inch" jelly-roll pan. Bake at three hundred fifty degrees for eighteen to twenty minutes, until edges pull away from sides of pan. Cool; spread with frosting and cut into bars. Arrange a few sliced gumdrops on each bar to look like a holly sprig. Prepares three dozen.

Chocolate-Caramel Pecan Bars

Ingredients

- 1-1/2 c. plus 3 T. all-purpose flour, divided
- 1/4 c. brown sugar, packed
- 3/4 c. caramel ice cream topping
- 1/2 c. plus 2 T. butter, softened and divided

- 3 eggs, beaten
- 3/4 c. light corn syrup
- 3/4 c. sugar
- 1 t. vanilla extract
- twelve-oz. pkg. semi-sweet chocolate chips
- 1-1/2 c. chopped pecans

Directions

1. Using an electric blender over medium speed, Combine one and half flour, half cup butter and brown sugar till it turns crumbly. Press into a greased 13 inch x 9 inch baking pan. Bake at three hundred fifty degrees for twelve to fifteen minutes, until golden; place aside. Mix caramel topping and rest of the flour until mixture is fairly thick; place aside. Melt rest of the butter; cool gently. Whisk together eggs, corn syrup, sugar, melted butter and vanilla; Mix in chocolate chips and pecans. Pour over baked crust; sprinkle with caramel mixture. Bake for an extra twenty five to thirty minutes. Cut into squares. Prepares two and half dozen

Heavenly Angel Bars

Ingredients

- sixteen-oz. pkg. graham crackers, divided
- 3/4 c. milk, divided
- 1 c. sugar
- 1-1/2 c. margarine, divided
- 1-1/2 t. vanilla extract, divided
- 1 c. sweetened flaked coconut
- 1 c. chopped pecans
- 1 egg, beaten
- 8-oz. can crushed pineapple, drained
- sixteen-oz. pkg. powdered sugar
- 1/2 t. butter flavoring

Directions

1. Crush enough crackers to equal one cup; place aside. Mix sugar, half cup milk, one cup margarine, one teaspoon vanilla and egg in a saucepan over medium flame; bring to a boil. Take off of flame; Put in coconut, crushed crackers, pecans and pineapple. Line baking sheet with half of rest of the whole crackers; spread warm mixture over top. Top with rest of the whole crackers, arranged in similar direction as bottom layer; place aside. Mix powdered sugar, butter flavoring, rest of the margarine and rest of the vanilla in a large bowl. Put in enough of rest of the milk to attain a spreading consistency, about 2 teaspoons each time. Spread over top. Refrigerate for at least two hours prior to slicing with perforations of crackers. Prepares three to four dozen.

Chocolate Thumbprints

Ingredients

- sixteen-oz. container chocolate frosting
- 2-1/2 c. graham cracker crumbs
- 1/4 c. butter, softened

- 1/2 t. almond extract
- 1 c. almonds, ground
- 48 milk chocolate drops, unwrapped

Directions

1. Mix frosting and butter in a large bowl; beat till it is properly blended. Mix in graham cracker crumbs and almond extract. Spread almonds in a shallow bowl; place aside. Shape chocolate mixture into 1-inch balls; roll in ground almonds to provide a coat. Set balls on ungreased baking sheets. Form a deep thumbprint indentation in the center of each ball; top using a chocolate drop. Refrigerate for thirty minutes, or till properly chilled. Prepares 4 dozen.

Grandma's Springerle

Ingredients

- 4 eggs
- 2 c. sugar
- 4 c. all-purpose flour
- 2 T. butter, softened
- 2 t. baking powder
- 1/4 t. salt
- 1/4 c. anise seed

Directions

1. Beat eggs in a large bowl until very light. Put in butter and sugar; beat till it turns fluffy. Mix flour, baking powder and salt in a different large bowl; Gradually insert in to butter mixture. Knead dough till it turns smooth, Put in more flour if required. Cover and let it cool for at least two hours. Using a plain rolling pin, roll out half-inch thick on a gently floured surface. Roll again using a springerle rolling pin to form designs. Cut cookies apart on lines marked by rolling pin. Drizzle gently anise seed on a neat tea towel; set cookies on towel, molded-side down. Allow to stand, uncovered, overnight. Place cookies on gently greased baking sheets. Bake at three hundred twenty five degrees for twelve to fifteen minutes; cool entirely. Keep in mind to store only in an airtight container. Cookies will Uniformly soften and develop stronger anise flavor. Prepares five dozen.

Pizzelles

Ingredients

- 6 eggs, beaten
- 1 c. butter, melted
- 1-1/2 c. sugar
- 4 t. baking powder
- 2 T. anise extract
- 2 T. vanilla extract
- 3-1/2 c. all-purpose flour
- Garnish: powdered sugar

Directions

1. Combine all ingredients excluding flour and powdered sugar till it turns creamy. Put in flour Uniformly; mix properly to form a very sticky dough. Drop dough according to teaspoonfuls onto a hot pizzelle iron. Bake for thirty to thirty five seconds until golden. Dust with powdered sugar. Prepares about five dozen.

Date Sandwich Cookies

Ingredients

- 3 c. long-cooking oats, uncooked
- 1 t. baking powder
- 1/4 t. salt
- 2-1/2 c. all-purpose flour
- 2 c. brown sugar, packed and divided
- 1/2 c. margarine, melted
- 1/2 c. butter, melted
- 1/2 c. milk
- 16-oz. pkg. chopped dates
- 1 c. hot water

Directions

1. Combine oats, flour, baking powder, one cup brown sugar, margarine, salt, butter and milk. Divide dough into four portions. On a floured surface, roll out 1 portion each time to about one by eight-inch thick. Cut out shapes using a glass or round cookie cutter. Transfer to greased baking sheets. Bake at three hundred twenty five degrees for ten to fifteen minutes. Remove to cool entirely. To form filling, Mix dates, rest of the brown sugar and hot water over medium flame. Cook for three to five minutes, until thickened. Cool entirely. Spread onto half of cookies; place another one on top. Prepares two dozen large cookies or three and half dozen small cookies.

Rugelach Cookies

Ingredients

- 1/2 c. chopped dates
- 1/3 c. plus 2 T. powdered low-calorie sugar mix for baking, divided
- 3 t. cinnamon, divided
- 1/2 c. pistachios, chopped
- 1/4 c. butter, softened
- 3 8-oz. tubes refrigerated crescent rolls

Directions

1. Mix dates, pistachios, one third cup sugar blend, two teaspoons cinnamon and butter in a medium bowl; mix properly and place aside. Separate crescent rolls. Drop 1 teaspoon date mixture onto every crescent roll; roll up. Arrange rolls on ungreased baking sheets. Bake at three hundred seventy five degrees for fourteen to eighteen minutes, until golden. Take off and place over a wire rack. Mix rest of the sugar mix and cinnamon; Drizzle gently over cookies. Prepares two dozen

Coconut Yule Cylinders

Ingredients

- 1-1/2 c. sweetened flaked coconut, divided
- 3 c. powdered sugar
- 1/2 t. vanilla extract
- 8-oz. pkg. cream cheese, softened
- 2 c. quick-cooking oats, uncooked
- 1/2 c. chopped almonds

Directions

1. Spread one cup coconut on a baking sheet. Bake at three hundred twenty five degrees for eight to ten minutes, tossing occasionally, until toasted. Place aside to cool. Beat cream cheese in a large bowl till it turns creamy. Uniformly put in powdered sugar, blending well; Put in vanilla. Mix in oats, rest of the coconut and almonds. Shape to Make two-inch cylinders; roll cylinders in toasted coconut. Keep in mind to store only in an airtight container; Make sure to refrigerate only until prepare to serve. Prepares three dozen

Holly Wreaths

Ingredients

- 1/2 c. butter
- 1/4 to 1 t. green food coloring
- thirty marshmallows
- 4-1/2 c. corn flake cereal
- 1/3 c. red cinnamon candies

Directions

1. Melt butter in a large saucepan over low flame; Put in marshmallows and mix till melts entirely. Put in food coloring; mix properly. Gently Mix in cereal to coat well. Transfer according to teaspoonfuls to greased aluminium foil; Prepare into wreath shapes. Decorate using cinnamon candies for holly berries while still warm. Prepares one to one and a half dozen.

Almond Candy Canes

Ingredients

- 1 c. butter, softened
- 1/4 t. salt
- 1 t. almond extract
- 2-1/2 c. powdered sugar, divided
- 1 c. chopped almonds
- 2 c. all-purpose flour
- 2 to 3 T. milk
- 4 to 6 candy canes, crushed

Directions

1. Mix butter, half cup powdered sugar, salt and extract in a large bowl. Using an electric blender on medium-high speed, beat till it turns fluffy. Mix in almonds and flour till it is properly blended. Roll

dough by heaping tablespoonfuls into a rope; shape them into candy canes. Set on a buttered or parchment paper-lined baking sheet. Bake at three hundred fifty degrees till they attain a golden hue, about fifteen to eighteen minutes. Cool on baking sheet until gently firm; carefully take off and place over a wire rack and cool entirely. Mix together rest of the powdered sugar and milk. Sprinkle frosting over cookies and Drizzle gently with crushed candy. Prepares about two dozen.

Popcorn Balls

Ingredients

- 5 qts. popped popcorn
- 1-1/2 c. water
- 1/2 t. salt
- 2 c. sugar
- 1/2 c. light corn syrup
- 1 t. vinegar
- 1 t. vanilla extract
- 16 to 20 candy canes

Directions

1. Keep popped corn in a large roaster; keep warm and crisp in a three hundred-degree oven. Butter the inner surface of a medium saucepan; Put in rest of the ingredients excluding vanilla and candy canes. Cook to hard-ball stage, two hundred fifty to two hundred seventy degrees on a candy thermometer; Put in vanilla. Pour slowly over popped corn, stirring just adequately to mix properly. Butter hands gently; shape popcorn mixture into an orange-size ball around straight end of every candy cane. Once cooled, place balls candy cane-side up on a plate. Prepares fifteen to twenty.

Date Pinwheels

Ingredients

- 16-oz. pkg. dates, chopped
- 1/2 c. sugar
- 1/2 t. vanilla extract
- 1/2 c. water
- 1 t. cinnamon, divided
- 1 c. butter-flavored shortening
- 2 c. brown sugar, packed
- 3 eggs
- 4 c. all-purpose flour
- 1 t. baking soda
- 1/2 t. salt

Directions

1. Mix dates, water and sugar in a medium saucepan over medium flame; cook until thickened. Mix in vanilla and half teaspoon cinnamon; cool. Mix shortening and brown sugar in a large bowl; Put in eggs, one each time, beating properly after each. In a separate large bowl, Combine flour, baking soda, salt and rest of the cinnamon. Uniformly Put in flour mixture to shortening mixture; Stir properly. Roll out half the dough to a one by four-inch thick rectangle. Spread half of cooled date

filling onto dough. Roll up jelly-roll style, beginning with the long end. Repeat with rest of the dough and filling to form a second roll. Wrap rolls in plastic wrap; Let cool for three to four hours to overnight. Slice dough into one fourths-inch slices; Make sure to arrange them on greased baking sheets. Bake at three hundred twenty five degrees for ten to twelve minutes. Prepares six dozen.

Polish Cookie Balls

Ingredients

- 1 c. butter, softened
- 2 c. all-purpose flour
- 1 t. vanilla extract
- 1/4 c. sugar
- 1 c. pecans, finely chopped
- 1 c. powdered sugar

Directions

1. Mix butter, sugar, flour and vanilla in a large bowl till it is properly blended; Mix in pecans. Prepare into 1-inch balls; Make sure to arrange them on ungreased baking sheets. Bake at three hundred twenty five degrees for twenty to twenty five minutes. Roll in powdered sugar while still warm. Prepares about two and half dozen.

Almond Cream Spritz

Ingredients

- 1 c. butter, softened
- 1/2 t. almond extract
- 3-oz. pkg. cream cheese, softened
- 1/2 c. sugar
- 1/4 t. vanilla extract
- 2 c. all-purpose flour
- 1/2 c. almonds, finely chopped

Directions

1. Beat combined butter and cream cheese in a large mixing bowl till properly blended. Put in sugar, almond extract and vanilla; mix properly. Mix in flour. Cover and chill dough for thirty minutes, or until easy enough to handle. Transfer dough to a cookie press. Press out cookies onto ungreased baking sheets; Drizzle gently using almonds. Bake at three hundred seventy five degrees for eight to ten minutes, until edges of cookies are golden. Remove to wire racks to cool. Prepares five dozen.

Noels

Ingredients

- 1 lb. walnut halves
- 1/3 c. plus 2 T. butter, softened and divided
- 3/4 c. brown sugar, packed
- 2 lbs. pitted whole dates
- 1 egg, beaten

- 2 t. vanilla extract, divided
- 1-1/4 c. all-purpose flour
- 1/2 t. baking soda
- 1/4 t. baking powder
- 1/2 t. salt
- 1/2 c. plus 1 T. sour cream, divided
- 1 c. powdered sugar

Directions

1. Insert a walnut into each date; place aside. Mix one third cup butter, brown sugar, egg, one teaspoon vanilla and flour; mix properly. Mix in baking soda, baking powder and half cup sour cream. Immerse dates in batter; Make sure to arrange them on smooth greased baking sheets. Bake at three hundred fifty degrees till they attain a golden hue, about three to four minutes. Cool entirely. Mix powdered sugar and rest of the butter, vanilla and sour cream; spread on cookies. Prepares about three dozen.

Coffee Eggnog

Ingredients

- 1 qt. eggnog
- 3/4 c. coffee liqueur or cooled brewed coffee
- Garnish: whipped topping, nutmeg

Directions

1. Mix eggnog and liqueur or coffee in a one and half quart pitcher. Pour into small glasses. Top with whipped topping and drizzle gently with nutmeg. Prepares eight servings.

Gingerbread Cottage

Ingredients

- 1/2-pint empty milk carton, washed
- graham crackers, broken into squares
- Royal Icing
- Garnish: mini candies, cereals, mini pretzels, sprinkles and other holiday
- treats
- Optional: decorator frosting tubes

Directions

1. Secure milk carton to a square of cardboard using a dab of Royal Icing. Grease gently the icing on sides of carton using a brush; place while pushing crackers firmly onto carton. Repeat for roof, using two crackers. To make the sides of roof, use a serrated knife to slice a cracker in 1/2 over the diagonal; press onto icing. Make windows and doors with mentioned garnishes, using icing to attach. Spread icing around house to appear like snowdrifts. If required, put in accents using colored decorator frosting. Prepares 1 cottage.

Royal Icing

Ingredients

- 1 pasteurized egg white
- 1-1/2 c. powdered sugar

Directions

1. Mix ingredients in a large bowl. Beat using an electric blender over high speed till they start to make stiff peaks. Prepares about three fourths cup

Cinnamon Hard Candy

Ingredients

- 1/2 c. powdered sugar
- 1-1/2 c. light corn syrup
- 1 c. water
- 3-3/4 c. sugar
- 1 t. cinnamon flavoring
- 1/2 to 1 t. red food coloring

Directions

1. Line a baking sheet with aluminium foil; Drizzle gently with powdered sugar and place aside. Mix sugar, corn syrup and water in a large saucepan over medium flame, mixing till sugar dissolves completely. Bring mixture to a boil without stirring till the point it attains the hard-crack stage, or two hundred ninety to three hundred ten degrees on a candy thermometer. Mix in flavoring and food coloring. Pour hot candy over prepared baking sheet. Allow to cool; break into pieces. Prepares about three pounds.

Candy Strawberries

Ingredients

- 2 3-oz. pkgs. strawberry gelatin mix
- 1 c. pecans, finely chopped
- 1 c. sweetened flaked coconut
- 1/2 c. sweetened condensed milk
- 1 t. vanilla extract
- red and green decorating sugar
- 1/3 c. slivered almonds
- few drops green food coloring

Directions

1. Beat together gelatin mixes and condensed milk in a large bowl till it turns smooth. Put in pecans, coconut and vanilla; stir just till combined properly. Make their shape like strawberries; roll sides of strawberries in red sugar and immerse tops into green sugar. Tint almonds using green food coloring and insert 1 into the top of every berry for the stem. Keep in mind to only store in an airtight container in refrigerator. Prepares two dozen.

Sparkling Sugarplums

Ingredients

- 1 c. dried apricots
- 1/2 c. golden raisins
- 1/2 c. pitted dates
- 1 c. pecans
- 2 c. vanilla wafers, crushed
- 1 c. sweetened flaked coconut
- 1/2 c. orange juice
- 1/2 c. sugar

Directions

1. Put after neatly chopping dates, apricots, raisins and pecans in a food processor. Mix with wafer crumbs in a big bowl; toss along coconut and orange juice. Prepare into three by four-inch balls; roll in sugar and set them in paper mini muffin liners. Prepares about four dozen

Oh-So-Easy Cut-Outs

Ingredients

- 17-1/2 oz. pkg. sugar cookie mix
- 1/3 c. butter, melted
- 2 T. all-purpose flour
- 1 egg, beaten
- Garnish: decorator gel tubes in desired colors

Directions

1. Mix together cookie mix, flour, butter and egg. Chill briefly in case very soft. Roll dough out one by four-inch thick on a gently floured surface. Cut out with cookie cutters. Set the cookies one inch apart from each other on ungreased baking sheets. Decorate unbaked cookies using decorator gels. Bake at three hundred seventy five degrees for eight to nine minutes, till they attain a golden hue around edges. Cool for one minute prior to removing from baking sheets; cool entirely. Prepares two dozen.

Italian Knot Cookies

Ingredients

- 6 T. butter, softened
- 1/2 t. salt
- 1/4 c. milk
- 1/3 c. sugar
- 1 egg
- 1 egg yolk
- 2 T. orange juice
- 2 t. orange zest
- 2 t. lemon zest
- 1 t. rum extract
- 4 t. lemon juice

- 2-1/2 c. all-purpose flour
- oil for deep-frying
- Garnish: powdered sugar

Directions

1. Process butter, salt and sugar in a food processor till it turns smooth. Put in milk, egg, egg yolk, juices, zests and extract; process till it turns smooth. Put in flour; pulse till properly combined. Turn dough out on a gently floured surface; knead until soft but not sticky. Fold in plastic wrap. Let it cool for at least thirty minutes, until dough is easy to handle. Divide dough in 1/2. On a gently floured surface, roll out one-half each time into a sixteen-inch by sixteen-inch square. Using a fluted pastry cutter or a knife, cut dough into ten strips, one and half inches wide. Slice strips in half crosswise. Tie each strip using a loose knot in the center; set on wax paper-lined baking sheets. Heat quite a few inches of oil to three hundred fifty degrees in a large saucepan. Fry six to seven knots each time for five minutes, until golden, turning halfway through. Drain on paper towels; cool entirely. Drizzle gently with powdered sugar. Prepares about three and half dozen.

Chocolate-Almond Fingers

Ingredients

- 1/2 c. plus 2 T. butter, softened and divided
- 1/3 c. cornstarch
- 1/4 c. brown sugar, packed
- 1 c. all-purpose flour
- 1/3 c. almonds, ground
- 1 t. vanilla extract
- 1/4 t. almond extract
- 4 1-oz. sqs. semi-sweet baking chocolate, chopped
- 1/3 c. chopped almonds

Directions

1. Mix half cup butter, flour, cornstarch, brown sugar, ground almonds and extracts; mix till the dough is formed. Divide dough into four equal shares. Roll each portion into a twelve to fourteen-inch rope about inch-inch in diameter. Cut each rope into two-inch lengths; Make sure to arrange them on_ ungreased baking sheets. Bake at three hundred fifty degrees for eighteen to twenty minutes, just until golden on bottom. Place on a wire rack to cool. Take chocolate in a microwave-safe container. Microwave over high setting for one to two minutes until melted; stir till it turns smooth. Immerse half of each cookie into melted chocolate, then into chopped almonds. Set placed on a wire rack over wax paper to harden. Prepares about two and half dozen.

Almond Sandies

Ingredients

- 3/4 c. sugar, divided
- 3/4 c. almonds
- 1-1/2 c. butter, chopped and softened
- 1/2 t. salt
- 4 t. vanilla extract

- 1/3 t. almond extract
- 3 c. all-purpose flour
- 3/4 c. coarse white or colored decorating sugar

Directions

1. Mix half cup sugar and salt in a food processor; process until very fine, about thirty to sixty seconds. Put in almonds; process until finely chopped, about twenty seconds. Put in butter and extracts; pulse till it turns smooth. Put in flour and pulse until a soft dough forms; spoon into a large bowl and mix properly. Work in rest of the sugar using a spoon. On a floured surface, shape dough into three cylinders, each six inches long by one to three by four inches in diameter. Wrap in wax paper; refrigerate for at least two hours. Spread coarse sugar uniformly over a flat surface. Roll dough cylinders in sugar to coat well. Slice cylinders one by four-inch thick; arrange one inch apart on ungreased baking sheets. Bake at three hundred fifty degrees for twelve to fifteen minutes. Allow to stand on baking sheets for two minutes; transfer to a wire rack to cool entirely. Keep in mind to store in an airtight container. Prepares about six dozen.

Cinnamon-Sugar Pinwheels

Ingredients

- 1/2 c. butter, softened
- 1 egg yolk
- 1 c. all-purpose flour
- 3-oz. pkg. cream cheese, softened
- 1/4 c. butter, melted
- 1/3 c. sugar
- 2 t. cinnamon
- 1/2 c. nuts, finely chopped
- Garnish: powdered sugar

Directions

1. Mix butter and cream cheese; Mix till it turns smooth. Mix in egg yolk and flour; mix properly. Cover and chill for thirty minutes. Divide dough in half; roll very thin, about one by eight-inch thick. Brush with melted butter; place aside. Mix sugar, cinnamon and nuts; Drizzle gently over dough. Roll up jelly-roll style, beginning at long edge. Slice rolls into half-inch slices; Make sure to arrange them on ungreased baking sheets. Repeat with rest of the dough. Bake at three hundred fifty degrees for fifteen minutes, or until golden. Remove to wire rack and cool; Drizzle gently with powdered sugar. Prepares two to three to three dozen.

Pastel Cream Wafers

Ingredients

- 2 c. all-purpose flour
- 1/3 c. whipping cream
- 1-1/2 c. butter, divided
- 2 c. sugar
- 2-1/3 c. powdered sugar
- 1 t. vanilla extract

- quite a few drops red food coloring

Directions

1. Mix flour, one cup butter and cream; mix properly. Allow to cool for 1 hour. Roll out dough to one by eight-inch thick; cut out cookies using a one and half inch round cookie cutter. Carefully Immerse both sides of cookies into sugar; set on a parchment paper-lined baking sheet. Pierce cookies gently across top using a fork. Bake at three hundred seventy five degrees for eight to nine minutes. Cool entirely. Beat rest of the butter for thirty seconds; Uniformly beat in powdered sugar, vanilla and food coloring. Sandwich cookies two at a time with frosting. Prepares about five dozen.

Two-Tone Icebox Cookies

Ingredients

- 1 c. butter, softened
- 1 egg
- 1 egg yolk
- 1 c. sugar
- 1 t. vanilla extract
- 2-3/4 c. all-purpose flour
- 2 T. baking cocoa

Directions

1. In a large bowl, Mix together butter and sugar. Gently beat in an egg, yolk and vanilla. Uniformly put in flour. Divide dough into two equal portions. Beat cocoa into one portion. Make dough into two rolls. Wrap dough in plastic wrap; refrigerate for at least four hours. Cut into one by four-inch slices; arrange one inch apart from each other on gently greased baking sheets. Bake at three hundred fifty degrees for eight to ten minutes. Prepares two dozen.

Bull's Eye Cookie s :

Wrap a dough rectangle of one color around a dough log of different color. It's entertaining to form half the cookies with dark dough centers, the other half with bright dough centers. Follow instructions mentioned above for refrigerating dough, slicing and baking.

Jam Turnovers

Ingredients

- 3-oz. pkg. cream cheese
- 1/8 t. salt
- 1/2 c. butter, softened
- 1 c. all-purpose flour
- twelve-oz. jar red raspberry jam or preserves

Directions

1. Mix cream cheese and butter together; Mix in flour and salt. Roll out on a floured surface. Cut out circles using a two-inch round cookie cutter. Put a teaspoonful of jam or preserves in the center of each circle. Fold over and press edges together using a fork to close properly. Place on ungreased

baking sheets. Bake at three hundred seventy five degrees for ten to fifteen minutes. Prepares sixteen to twenty.

Viennese Crescents

Ingredients

- 2 c. all-purpose flour
- 1 c. hazelnuts, ground
- 2-1/2 c. powdered sugar, divided
- 1 c. butter, softened
- 1/8 t. salt
- 1 t. vanilla extract
- 1 T. vanilla-flavored powdered non-dairy creamer

Directions

1. Mix flour, butter, nuts, half cup powdered sugar, salt and vanilla. Mix by hand till it is properly blended. Cover and Allow to cool for 1 hour. Shape dough into 1-inch balls; roll each ball into a small roll three inches long and curve to make a crescent outline. Make sure to place them two inches from each other on ungreased baking sheets. Bake at three hundred seventy five degrees for ten to twelve minutes, or until golden and set. Allow to stand for one minute; Take off of cookie sheets. Mix rest of the powdered sugar and creamer. Drizzle gently hot cookies with powdered sugar mixture; turn gently to coat on both sides. Let cool and store in an airtight container. Prepares two dozen.

Golden Tassies

Ingredients

- 1 c. margarine, softened
- 2 c. all-purpose flour
- 1 c. pecans, finely chopped and divided
- 2 3-oz. pkgs. cream cheese, softened
- 3 eggs, beaten
- 3 T. margarine, melted
- 2-1/4 c. brown sugar, packed
- 2 t. vanilla extract
- 1/2 t. salt

Directions

1. Combine softened margarine and cream cheese; Uniformly put in flour. Mix properly; refrigerate for thirty minutes or longer. Press 1-inch balls of dough into ungreased mini muffin tins, shaping with floured fingers. Drizzle gently about one teaspoon chopped pecans into each muffin cup. Mix eggs, melted margarine, vanilla, brown sugar and salt, beating till it turns smooth. Pour over nuts. Drizzle gently rest of the nuts over top. Bake at three hundred twenty five degrees for twenty five to thirty minutes. Prepares three to four dozen.

Caramel-Coffee Tassies

Ingredients

- 3-oz. pkg. cream cheese, softened
- 1 c. all-purpose flour
- fourteen-oz. pkg. caramels, unwrapped
- 1/2 c. butter, softened
- 1/4 c. evaporated milk
- 1-1/2 t. coffee liqueur or brewed coffee

Directions

1. Beat combined cream cheese and butter till they are properly blended; Mix in flour. Prepare into a ball; Allow to cool for 1 hour to overnight. Shape dough into half-inch balls; press each into a ungreased mini muffin tin. Bake at three hundred fifty degrees for ten to fifteen minutes, until golden. Allow to cool. Mix caramels and evaporated milk in a saucepan over medium flame. Stir frequently until melted. Take off of flame; Mix in liqueur or coffee. Spoon caramel filling into baked shells; Allow to cool. Pipe frosting onto caramel filling. Prepares about two dozen

Frosting:

- 1 c. shortening
- 2/3 c. sugar
- 2/3 c. evaporated milk, chilled
- 1 t. coffee liqueur or brewed coffee

Mix shortening and sugar together till it turns fluffy; Put in evaporated milk and liqueur or coffee. Beat Using an electric blender on medium-high till it turns fluffy, about eight to ten minutes.

Grandma's Butter Fingers

Ingredients

- 1 c. chopped pecans
- 3/4 c. sugar
- 1 c. butter, softened
- 2-1/2 c. all-purpose flour
- 1 t. vanilla extract
- sixteen-oz. pkg. powdered sugar

Directions

1. Mix all ingredients excluding powdered sugar and mix properly. Make dough into small fingers or cylinders; et on an ungreased baking sheet. Bake at three hundred twenty five degrees for twenty to thirty minutes. Immediately roll in powdered sugar to coat. Prepares about eight dozen.

Peppermint Biscotti

Ingredients

- 3/4 c. butter, softened
- 3 eggs
- 2 t. peppermint extract
- 3-1/4 c. all-purpose flour

- 3/4 c. sugar
- 1 t. baking powder
- 1/4 t. salt
- 2 c. semi-sweet chocolate chips
- 1-1/2 c. candy canes, crushed and divided
- 2 T. shortening

Directions

1. Mix butter and sugar. Put in eggs, one each time, beating properly after each addition; Mix in extract. Mix flour, baking powder, salt and one cup crushed candy in a different bowl. Uniformly Put in flour mixture to butter mixture, mixing well to a stiff dough. Divide dough in half. Roll each half into a twelve-inch by two and a half-inch rectangle; place on ungreased baking sheets. Bake at three hundred fifty degrees for twenty five to thirty minutes, until golden. Carefully remove to wire racks; cool for fifteen minutes. Place on a cutting board; using a sharp knife, slice 1/2-inch thick on the diagonal. Return slices to baking sheets, cut-side down. Bake an Put in extra twelve to fifteen minutes, till it turns stiff. Place on a wire rack to cool. In a microwave-safe bowl, melt chocolate chips and shortening; stir till it turns smooth. Immerse one end of each cookie into melted chocolate; roll in rest of the crushed candy. Set on wax paper till they are well set. Keep in mind to store only in an airtight container. Prepares about three and half dozen.

French Madeleines

Ingredients

- 2 eggs, beaten
- 1/2 t. lemon zest
- 1 c. powdered sugar
- 1/2 t. vanilla extract
- 3/4 c. all-purpose flour
- 1/4 t. baking powder
- 1/2 c. butter, melted and cooled
- Garnish: powdered sugar

Directions

1. Beat eggs, vanilla and lemon zest for five minutes Using an electric blender over high speed. Uniformly put in powdered sugar. Beat for six to seven minutes, until thick and glossy; place aside. Mix together flour and baking powder. Put in one fourth of flour mixture to egg mixture and lightly fold in using a spoon; Uniformly fold in rest of the flour. Mix in butter. Spoon batter into twenty five greased and floured three-inch madeleine molds, filling three fourths full. Bake at three hundred seventy five degrees for ten to twelve minutes, till the edges attain a golden hue. Keep molds on a rack to cool for 1 minute. Loosen edges using a knife; Place cookies on a wire rack to cool. Drizzle gently with powdered sugar. Keep stored in an airtight container. Prepares two dozen.

Raspberry Linzer Tarts

Ingredients

- 1-1/4 c. butter, softened
- 1-3/4 c. almonds, ground

- 2/3 c. sugar
- 1/8 t. cinnamon
- 2 c. all-purpose flour
- 6 T. raspberry jam
- Garnish: powdered sugar

Directions

1. Mix butter and sugar till they turn fluffy and light. Mix in almonds, cinnamon and flour, half cup each time. Cover and refrigerate for about one hour. On a gently floured surface, roll out half of dough one by eight-inch thick. Cut out twenty five circles using a two and a half-inch round cookie cutter. Cut out centers of twelve circles using a half-inch mini cookie cutter; leave rest of the twelve circles uncut. Arrange one inch apart on ungreased baking sheets. Bake at three hundred twenty five degrees for ten to fifteen minutes, until golden. Cool entirely placed on a wire rack. Spread jam in thin layers over solid circles; sandwich each using a cut-out cookie. Spoon a bit of rest of the jam into cut-outs; Drizzle gently with powdered sugar. Prepares one dozen.

Cream-Filled Pecan Snaps

Ingredients

- 3 T. butter, melted
- 2 T. dark corn syrup
- 1 T. coffee liqueur or brewed coffee
- 1/4 c. brown sugar, packed
- 1/2 c. pecans, finely chopped
- 1/4 c. all-purpose flour
- 1/4 c. powdered sugar
- 1 c. whipping cream
- 4 t. instant espresso coffee
- Optional: grated chocolate

Directions

1. Mix butter, brown sugar, corn syrup and coffee liqueur or coffee in a small bowl. Mix in pecans and flour till combined properly. Drop onto gently greased baking sheets according to tablespoons, five inches apart. Bake at three hundred fifty degrees for eight to ten minutes, until bubbly and golden. Make use of baking sheets for cooling for one to two minutes. Quickly roll each cookie around a metal cone or a wooden spoon handle; slide off. Cool entirely placed on a wire rack. Shortly prior to serving, Mix cream, powdered sugar and espresso powder. Beat Using an electric blender over low speed till they start to Make stiff peaks. Place using a spoon into a plastic zipping bag; snip off one corner and pipe into cookies. Dust with grated chocolate, if required. Prepares about two and half dozen.

Pecan Icebox Cookies

Ingredients

- 1-1/2 c. butter, softened
- 1 c. brown sugar, packed
- 2 eggs, beaten

- 1 t. baking soda
- 1 c. sugar
- 2 t. vanilla extract
- 1/8 t. salt
- 4 c. all-purpose flour
- 1 t. cream of tartar
- 1 c. chopped pecans

Directions

1. Combine butter, sugars and eggs till it turns creamy. Put in rest of the ingredients excluding pecans; mix properly. Mix in pecans and prepare into three to four cylinders two inches wide. Roll each cylinder in wax paper, covering well; Allow to cool for 1 hour to overnight. Slice one by four-inch thick and make sure to arrange them on ungreased baking sheets. Bake at three hundred fifty degrees for eight to ten minutes. Prepares six to eight dozen.

Chocolate Cherry Delights

Ingredients

- 1/4 c. butter, melted
- twelve maraschino cherries, finely chopped
- 2/3 c. creamy peanut butter
- 2 c. powdered sugar
- 1 c. chopped walnuts
- 1 c. sweetened flaked coconut
- 1/8 t. salt
- 6-oz. pkg. semi-sweet chocolate chips
- 3-1/2 T. paraffin, chopped

Directions

1. Combine all ingredients excluding chocolate chips and paraffin. Prepare into 1-inch balls; place aside. Melt chocolate chips and paraffin in a double boiler over medium-low flame till it turns smooth. Immerse balls into chocolate mixture to coat; Allow to stand on wax paper till they are well set. Prepares about two and half dozen.

Devil's Food Cookies

Ingredients

- eighteen-1/2 oz. pkg. devil's food cake mix
- 3/4 c. chopped pecans or walnuts
- twelve-oz. container frozen whipped topping, thawed
- 1 egg, beaten
- Garnish: powdered sugar

Directions

1. Mix all ingredients excluding powdered sugar in a large bowl; mix properly. Prepare into 1-inch balls; roll in powdered sugar. Bake at three hundred fifty degrees on an ungreased baking sheet for

ten to twelve minutes. Prepares four dozen.

Oatmeal Drop Cookies

Ingredients

- 2 c. sugar
- 1/2 c. milk
- 1/2 c. margarine
- 1/4 c. baking cocoa
- 3 c. quick-cooking oats, uncooked
- 1/4 c. creamy peanut butter
- 1 t. vanilla extract
- 1/8 t. salt

Directions

1. Mix sugar, cocoa, milk and margarine in a large saucepan over medium flame. Bring to a boil; cook for 1 minute. Take off of flame and put in oats, peanut butter, vanilla and salt; mix properly. Drop mixture according to teaspoonfuls onto wax paper. Allow to stand for two to three hours. Prepares about five dozen.

Peanut Butter Pinwheels

Ingredients

- 1 c. butter, softened
- 16-oz. pkg. powdered sugar
- Put extra powdered sugar for rolling out
- 1 c. creamy peanut butter

Directions

1. Mix butter and powdered sugar till properly mixed. Divide mixture into three balls. Using a rolling pin sprinkled with powdered sugar, roll out each ball into a one by eight-thick rectangle on wax paper sprinkled with crushed sugar. Put a thin layer of peanut butter on top. Beginning with long side of each rectangle, roll up jelly-roll style. Refrigerate for at least thirty minutes; slice three by four-inch thick. Prepares about two and half dozen.

Corny Crunch Bars

Ingredients

- 2 c. light corn syrup
- 2 c. crunchy peanut butter
- 2 c. sugar
- 2 9-3/4 oz. pkgs corn chips

Directions

1. Mix corn syrup and sugar in a saucepan over medium flame; bring to a boil. Take off of flame; Mix in peanut butter. Place corn chips in a large bowl coated with non-stick vegetable spray; Mix in peanut butter mixture. Gently press onto a buttered 18 inch x 12 inch baking pan and allow to cool.

Cut into squares. Prepares about two dozen.

Marbled Cheesecake Bars

Ingredients

- 18-3/4 oz. pkg. German chocolate cake mix
- 1/2 c. sugar
- 8-oz. pkg. cream cheese, softened
- 3/4 c. milk chocolate chips, divided

Directions

1. Make cake mix according to package instructions; pour into a greased 17 inch x 12 inch baking pan and place aside. Beat together cream cheese and sugar; Mix in one fourth cup chocolate chips. Transfer by tablespoonfuls over batter. Cut through batter using a knife to swirl cream cheese mixture; Drizzle gently with rest of the chocolate chips. Bake at three hundred fifty degrees for twenty five to thirty minutes, or till a toothpick inserted near center tests clean. Place over a wire rack to let the cool; slice into bars. Prepares about three dozen.

Peanut Butter Snowballs

Ingredients

- 2 c. creamy peanut butter
- 2 c. powdered sugar
- 2 c. crispy rice cereal
- 2 T. butter, softened
- sixteen-oz. pkg. white melting chocolate, chopped

Directions

1. Mix peanut butter, butter and powdered sugar. Put in cereal; mix properly. Shape into balls according to teaspoonfuls. Set balls on wax paper; freeze for few hours to overnight. Melt chocolate in a double boiler over medium-low flame; stir till it turns smooth. Immerse balls into melted chocolate; return to wax paper till they are well set. Prepares four to five dozen.

Merry Christmas Cookies

Ingredients

- 2 16-1/2 oz. tubes refrigerated sugar cookie dough, softened
- 1 c. pistachios, chopped
- 1 c. dried cherries, chopped
- 2 11-oz. pkgs. white chocolate chips

Directions

1. Mix cookie dough, cherries and pistachios in a large bowl; mix properly. Shape into two cylinders; Allow to cool for 1 hour. Slice cookies one by four-inch thick; Make sure to arrange them on gently greased baking sheets. Bake at three hundred fifty degrees for twelve to fourteen minutes, until golden. Cool entirely. Melt chocolate in a double boiler over medium-low flame; stir till it turns smooth. Immerse cookies in melted chocolate and place on wax paper; Allow to stand till they are

well set. Prepares about five dozen.

Pecan Pie Bars

Ingredients

- 18-1/2 oz. pkg. yellow cake mix, divided
- 1 egg, beaten
- 1/2 c. brown sugar, packed
- 1/2 c. butter, melted
- 1-1/2 c. light corn syrup
- 3 eggs, beaten
- 1 t. vanilla extract
- 1 c. chopped pecans

Directions

1. Place aside two third cup dry cake mix for filling. In a large bowl, Mix rest of the cake mix, butter and egg; mix properly. Press into a greased 13 inch x 9 inch baking pan. Bake at three hundred fifty degrees for fifteen to twenty minutes, till they attain a golden hue; remove and place aside. In a large bowl, mix reserved cake mix, brown sugar, corn syrup, eggs and vanilla. Beat for two minutes using an electric blender over medium speed. Mix in pecans and pour over baked crust. Bake for thirty to thirty five minutes at three hundred fifty degrees, until almost set. Cool; slice into bars. Prepares about two dozen

Gingerbread Pinwheels

Ingredients

- 16-1/2 oz. tube refrigerated gingerbread cookie dough, halved lengthwise
- 16-1/2 oz. tube refrigerated sugar cookie dough, halved lengthwise

Directions

1. Keep gingerbread dough halves side-by-side on a wax paper-lined 15 inch x 10 inch jelly-roll pan. Roll or pat into a single 15 inch x 9-inch rectangle; freeze for five minutes. Replicate steps with sugar cookie dough. Lifting with wax paper kept at the bottom, turn over sugar cookie dough and place on top of gingerbread dough. Gently pat together the doughs; refrigerate fifteen minutes. Peel off wax paper on top. Beginning with one long side, roll up stacked dough jelly-roll style, peeling off bottom wax paper as dough is rolled. Wrap tightly inside more wax paper; freeze for forty five minutes. Unwrap dough and slice one by four-inch thick. Arrange slices two inches apart from each other on ungreased baking sheets. Bake at three hundred fifty degrees for ten to twelve minutes. Prepares four to five dozen.

Chewy Cereal Bars

Ingredients

- 1 c. sugar
- 1 c. light corn syrup
- 1 c. creamy peanut butter
- 1 t. vanilla extract

- 6 c. doughnut-shaped oat cereal

Directions

1. Mix together sugar and corn syrup in a saucepan over medium flame; boil for 1 minute. Take off of flame; Put in peanut butter and vanilla, stirring till it turns smooth. Place cereal in a big bowl coated with non-stick cooking spray; Mix in peanut butter mixture. Press into a buttered 15 inch x 10 inch jelly roll pan and allow to cool. Cut into squares. Prepares two to three dozen

Club Cracker Goodie Bars

Ingredients

- 60 rectangular buttery crackers, divided
- 1/3 c. milk
- 1/2 c. sugar
- 1/2 c. butter
- 3/4 c. brown sugar, packed
- 1 c. graham cracker crumbs
- 2/3 c. crunchy peanut butter
- 1 c. semi-sweet chocolate chips
- 1/2 c. chopped peanuts

Directions

1. In a gently greased 13 inch x 9 inch baking pan, arrange half of crackers in a single layer; place aside. Melt butter in a saucepan over medium flame; Put in milk, sugars and graham cracker crumbs. Boil for five minutes; pour over crackers placed in the pan. Top with rest of the crackers. Melt chocolate chips and peanut butter in a saucepan over low flame, stirring continually until melted; spread over crackers. Drizzle gently with peanuts. Cover and refrigerate for three hours. Cut into bars; refrigerate until prepared to serve. Prepares about two and half dozen.

Butter Brickle Cookies

Ingredients

- eighteen-oz. pkg. butter pecan cake mix
- 1/2 c. margarine, softened
- 2 eggs, beaten
- 8-oz. pkg. toffee baking bits

Directions

1. Combine all ingredients. Transfer by tablespoonfuls onto greased baking sheets. Bake at three hundred fifty degrees for nine to ten minutes. Prepares three to four dozen.

Easy Almond Spritz

Ingredients

- 17-1/2 oz. pkg. sugar cookie mix
- 1 egg, beaten
- 1/2 c. all-purpose flour

- 1/2 c. butter, melted
- 1 t. almond extract
- Garnish: colored sugar, candy sprinkles

Directions

1. In a large bowl, mix together dry cookie mix, butter, egg, flour and extract till you witness a soft dough forming. Fill a cookie press with cookie dough; Set cookies on ungreased baking sheets. Decorate as desired with sugar or sprinkles. Bake at three hundred seventy five degrees for six to eight minutes, or till they are well set. Cool for 1 minute; Take off of baking sheets to wire rack. Prepares four dozen.

Peanut Butter Meltaways

Ingredients

- 8 1-oz. sqs. melting chocolate
- 1 T. shortening
- 8 1-oz. sqs. white melting chocolate
- 2-1/4 c. creamy peanut butter

Directions

1. Line a 13 inch x 9 inch baking pan using aluminium foil; spray with non-stick vegetable spray and place aside. In a large microwave-safe bowl, Mix chocolates and shortening. Microwave over high setting for thirty seconds each time until melted; stir till it turns smooth. Put in peanut butter to chocolate mixture and stir properly. Pour into prepared pan; Allow to cool for 1 hour. Cut into squares. Prepares two dozen.

Graham Kringles

Ingredients

- 24 cinnamon graham cracker squares
- 1/2 c. butter
- 1 c. brown sugar, packed
- 1/2 c. margarine
- 1 c. chopped pecans

Directions

1. Layer graham crackers in an aluminium foil-lined 15 inch x 10 inch jelly-roll pan. Melt butter, margarine and brown sugar in a saucepan over medium flame. Bring to a boil; simmer for two minutes. Pour over crackers; Drizzle gently with nuts. Bake at three hundred fifty degrees for ten to twelve minutes. Slice into triangles while still warm. Prepares four dozen.

Angel Meringues

Ingredients

- 5 egg whites
- 1-1/2 t. vanilla extract
- 1/3 c. powdered calorie-free sweetener

- 1/8 t. salt

Directions

1. Using an electric blender on medium-low speed, beat egg whites till they start to make froth. Put in sweetener, vanilla and salt. Mix over high speed till they start to make stiff peaks, about twenty to thirty seconds. Spoon by rounded tablespoonfuls onto a gently greased baking sheet. Bake at three hundred fifty degrees for ten to fifteen minutes, until golden. Take off of pan; cool. Prepares about one dozen.

Santa Cookies

Ingredients

- 1 c. powdered sugar
- 1/2 t. vanilla extract
- sixteen-oz. pkg. peanut-shaped sandwich cookies
- 4-1/4 oz. tube red decorator icing
- 2 T. milk
- Garnish: quartered mini marshmallows, mini semi-sweet chocolate chips,
- red cinnamon candies

Directions

1. Combine powdered sugar, milk and vanilla together for attaining a frosting consistency. Spread a small quantity of frosting on all ends of cookies, leaving center of cookies plain to decorate for Santa's face. Let frosting dry entirely on wire racks. Decorate top of each cookie using red icing to form a hat. Using white frosting to attach, put in a marshmallow quarter to hat for a pompom, two chocolate chip eyes and a cinnamon candy nose. Let cookies dry entirely placed on a wire rack prior to serving. Prepares about two and half dozen.

Quick Fruitcake Bites

Ingredients

- 2 c. mini marshmallows
- 1 c. maraschino cherries, chopped
- fourteen-oz. can sweetened condensed milk
- 2 c. graham cracker crumbs
- 1/2 c. chopped pecans
- 3 c. sweetened flaked coconut

Directions

1. Mix all ingredients excluding coconut; mix properly. Make dough into 1 inch balls; roll in coconut. Chill for three hours, or till it turns stiff. Make sure to refrigerate only in an airtight container. Prepares about five dozen.

Tropical Truffles

Ingredients

- 8-oz. pkg. cream cheese, softened

- 8-oz. can crushed pineapple, drained
- 2-1/2 c. sweetened flaked coconut

Directions

1. Beat together cream cheese and pineapple. Cover and refrigerate for thirty minutes. Prepare into 1-inch balls; roll in coconut. Refrigerate until prepared to serve. Prepares two dozen.

Connie's Sandwich Cookies

Ingredients

- 16-1/2 oz. tube refrigerated peanut butter cookie dough
- 1/2 c. creamy peanut butter
- 16-1/2 oz. tube refrigerated chocolate chip dough
- sixteen-oz. container chocolate frosting

Directions

1. Slice each tube of dough into thirty five equal pieces; roll into balls. Arrange balls two inches apart on ungreased baking sheets; flatten gently in a criss-cross pattern using a fork immersed in sugar. Bake at three hundred fifty degrees for eight to ten minutes, till they attain a golden hue. Place placed on a wire rack to cool. Stir peanut butter into frosting till it is properly blended; spread onto peanut butter cookies. Put in chocolate chip cookies to make sandwiches; press lightly. Let chill until serving time. Prepares three dozen.

1-2-3 Cookies

Ingredients

- 18-1/2 oz. pkg. favorite-flavor cake mix
- 1 egg, beaten
- 8-oz. container frozen whipped topping, thawed
- 1/2 c. powdered sugar

Directions

1. Combine all ingredients excluding powdered sugar; Prepare into 1-inch balls. Roll in powdered sugar; set on ungreased baking sheets. Bake at three hundred fifty degrees for twelve to fifteen minutes; cool. Prepares about six dozen.

Old-Time Skillet Cookies

Ingredients

- 1/2 c. butter
- 2 eggs, beaten
- 3/4 c. sugar
- 2 c. chopped dates
- 1 c. chopped pecans
- 1 t. vanilla extract
- 2 c. crispy rice cereal
- 3-1/2 oz. can sweetened flaked coconut

Directions

1. Mix butter, sugar and eggs in a large skillet over low flame; cook until butter is melted and sugar is well blended. Put in chopped dates and cook for an extra ten minutes. Take off of flame; Mix in pecans and vanilla. Cool for five to ten minutes; Put in cereal. Roll into walnut-size balls; roll in coconut. Keep in mind to store only in airtight container. Prepares three and half dozen.

Saucepan Cookies

Ingredients

- 1/2 c. butter
- 1/2 c. milk
- 2 c. sugar
- 2 1-oz. sqs. unsweetened baking chocolate
- 1/2 t. salt
- 1 t. vanilla extract
- 4 c. quick-cooking oats, uncooked

Directions

1. In a big saucepan over medium flame, melt butter and chocolate. Put in milk, sugar and salt. Allow to come to a boil; boil for two minutes. Take off of flame. Put in vanilla and oats; mix properly. Transfer by rounded tablespoonfuls onto wax paper to cool. Prepares about four to five dozen.

Butterscotch Crunchies

Ingredients

- 2 c. butterscotch chips
- 1/4 c. creamy peanut butter
- 3-1/2 c. corn flake cereal

Directions

1. Melt butterscotch chips in a big saucepan over low flame. Put in peanut butter; Mix in cereal. Transfer by tablespoonfuls onto wax paper; cool. Prepares two dozen.

Graham No-Bake Cookies

Ingredients

- 2 c. sugar
- 2 T. baking cocoa
- 1/2 c. butter
- 1/2 c. milk
- 1/2 c. creamy peanut butter
- 1 T. vanilla extract
- 2 c. quick-cooking oats, uncooked
- 1 c. graham cracker crumbs

Directions

1. Mix sugar, milk, cocoa and butter in a saucepan over medium flame. Bring to a boil for two minutes,

stirring continually. Take off of flame. Mix in peanut butter, vanilla, oats and crumbs; mix properly. Transfer by rounded tablespoonfuls onto buttered wax paper; cool entirely. Prepares four to five dozen.

Ladybug Cookies

Ingredients

- 18-1/2 oz. pkg. red velvet cake mix
- 2 eggs, beaten
- 1/2 c. oil
- twelve-oz. pkg. semi-sweet chocolate chips

Directions

1. Mix dry cake mix, oil and eggs; mix properly. Mix in chocolate chips; Transfer by tablespoonfuls onto ungreased baking sheets. Bake at three hundred fifty degrees for nine to ten minutes. Prepares three and half dozen.

Peanut Butter Surprise Cookies

Ingredients

- 1 c. creamy peanut butter
- 1 sleeve round buttery crackers
- 2 twelve-oz. pkgs. semi-sweet or milk chocolate chips

Directions

1. Apply one tablespoon peanut butter on each cracker; place aside. Keep chocolate chips in a microwave-safe bowl. Microwave over high setting for two to three minutes, stirring every fifteen seconds, until melted. With tongs, Immerse each cracker into melted chocolate, coating properly. Set on wax paper; Allow to cool and harden. Keep in mind to store only in an airtight container. Prepares two dozen.

Creamy Christmas Eggnog

Ingredients

- 4 pasteurized eggs, separated and divided
- 1 T. sugar
- 1 t. vanilla extract
- 5-oz. can evaporated milk
- 4-1/2 c. milk
- Optional: 2 T. rum

Directions

1. Beat egg yolks in a big bowl till the point they thicken and turn light. Uniformly mix in evaporated milk, sugar, vanilla and milk. Take a different bowl and beat egg whites till they start to make stiff peaks; Take in to milk mixture. Mix in rum, if desired. Prepares seven to eight servings.

Cocoa Mocha Bites

Ingredients

- 1/2 c. butter, softened
- 3 T. baking cocoa
- 2/3 c. sugar
- 1 T. strong brewed coffee
- 1/2 t. vanilla extract
- 1-3/4 c. quick-cooking oats, uncooked
- 1/3 c. powdered sugar

Directions

1. Mix together butter, coffee, sugar, cocoa and vanilla. Mix in oats; mix properly. Roll into 1-inch balls. Immerse balls into powdered sugar; place on wax paper to set. Prepares about three dozen.

Cinnamon Cornmeal Cookies

Ingredients

- 16-1/2 oz. tube refrigerated sugar cookie dough, softened
- 1/4 c. yellow cornmeal
- twenty mini chocolate candy bars
- 1/3 c. cinnamon baking chips
- 1 t. shortening

Directions

1. Take up cookie dough in a big bowl; knead in cornmeal till it is properly blended. Wrap every candy bar in a rounded tablespoonful of dough, covering entirely. Arrange two inches apart on slightly greased baking sheets. Bake at three hundred seventy five degrees for ten to twelve minutes, till the edges attain a golden hue. Make use of baking sheets for cooling for one minute; remove to wire rack and cool entirely. Mix cinnamon chips and shortening in a medium microwave-safe bowl. microwave over high setting for thirty to forty five seconds, stirring every fifteen minutes, till it turns smooth. Sprinkle over cookies; Allow to stand till they are well set. Prepares about one and a half dozen.

Peanut Butter & Jam Bars

Ingredients

- 17-1/2 oz. pkg. peanut butter cookie mix
- 1 T. water
- 1 egg, beaten
- 3 T. oil
- 1/2 c. peanut butter chips
- sixteen-oz. container vanilla frosting
- 1 T. milk
- 1/4 c. creamy peanut butter
- 1/4 c. strawberry jam

Directions

1. Combine cookie mix, oil, water and egg; Mix in with a soft dough. Put in chips and mix properly. Press dough into a gently greased 13 inch x 9 inch baking pan. Bake at three hundred fifty degrees for fifteen to eighteen minutes, until edges are light golden. Cool entirely, about thirty minutes. Mix frosting, milk and peanut butter together till it is properly blended. Spread over baked crust. Drop jam by teaspoonfuls over frosting mixture; swirl jam using a knife tip to form a marbled design. Refrigerate for twenty minutes, or till they are well set. Cut into bars. Prepares about three dozen.

Double Chocolate Brownies

Ingredients

- 1 c. chopped pecans
- 2 c. sugar
- 1-1/2 c. all-purpose flour, divided
- 10 T. baking cocoa, divided
- 1-1/2 c. margarine, melted and divided
- 4 eggs, beaten
- 1 t. vanilla extract
- 16-oz. pkg. powdered sugar
- 6 T. milk

Directions

1. Toss pecans using some quantity of the flour; place aside. Combine rest of the flour, sugar, five tablespoons cocoa, 1 cup margarine, eggs and vanilla. Mix in pecans; spread in a greased 11 inch x 7 inch baking pan. Bake at three hundred fifty degrees for thirty minutes. For icing, mix powdered sugar, milk, rest of the cocoa and rest of the margarine; mix till it turns smooth. Pour over brownies while still hot. Let cool; Cut into squares. Prepares two dozen.

Buckeye Brownies

Ingredients

- 3/4 c. all-purpose flour
- 1/2 t. salt
- 1/2 c. butter, softened and divided
- 1/2 t. baking powder
- 6 T. baking cocoa
- 1 c. sugar
- 2 eggs, beaten
- 1-1/2 t. vanilla extract, divided
- 1/2 c. creamy peanut butter
- 1-1/4 c. powdered sugar
- 1 c. milk chocolate chips

Directions

1. Line an 8inch x 8inch square baking pan with two crossed strips of aluminium foil; spray using non-stick vegetable spray and place aside. Mix flour, baking powder and salt; place aside. In a microwave-safe bowl, melt one third cup butter for 1 minute over high setting. Put in cocoa, sugar, eggs and one teaspoon vanilla; beat for 1 minute, till it is properly blended. Put in dry ingredients;

mix till combined properly. Spread in prepared pan. Bake at three hundred fifty degrees for twenty minutes. Take off of oven; Allow to stand for ten minutes. Mix peanut butter and rest of the butter. Put in powdered sugar and rest of the vanilla; mix till it turns smooth. Place mixture between two lengths of wax paper; roll out into an 8- inch x 8-inch square. Using foil strips as handles, take off brownies from pan; place aside. Peel off wax paper from top of peanut butter mixture; turn onto top of brownies. Peel off rest of the wax paper. Melt chocolate chips and spread over top. Chill till it turns stiff, about 1 hour. Slice into squares. Prepares one dozen.

Italian Chocolate Cookies

Ingredients

- 4 c. all-purpose flour
- 2 t. ground cloves
- 2 t. cinnamon
- 1/4 c. baking cocoa
- 2 t. nutmeg
- 2 T. baking powder
- 1/2 t. salt
- 1-1/2 c. sugar
- 1 t. vanilla extract
- 1/2 c. shortening, melted
- 1 c. warm brewed coffee
- 1 c. chopped nuts
- 1 c. raisins
- 1 c. powdered sugar
- 3 to 4 t. water

Directions

1. Mix flour, cocoa, baking powder, spices and salt; place aside. Take a different bowl and mix together shortening and sugar. Mix in vanilla extract and coffee; Uniformly put in flour mixture till properly mixed. Mix in nuts and raisins. Prepare_ into 1-inch balls and make sure to arrange them on slightly greased baking sheets. Bake at three hundred fifty degrees for ten minutes; Let cool. Combine powdered sugar and water; sprinkle over cookies. Prepares two to three dozen.

Layered Mint Chocolate Fudge

Ingredients

- 12-oz. pkg. semi-sweet chocolate chips
- 2 t. vanilla extract
- 6-oz. pkg. white chocolate chips
- 14-oz. can sweetened condensed milk, divided
- 1 T. peppermint extract
- few drops green or red food coloring

Directions

1. Melt semi-sweet chocolate chips along 1 cup condensed milk in a big saucepan over low flame. Mix in vanilla. Spread half the mixture in a wax paper-lined 8 inch x 8 inch baking pan; chill for ten

minutes, or till it turns stiff. Place aside from rest of the chocolate mixture at room temperature. In another heavy saucepan over low flame, melt white chocolate chips with rest of the condensed milk. Mix in extract and desired food coloring. Spread over cooled chocolate layer; chill for ten minutes, or till it turns stiff. Spread reserved chocolate mixture over mint layer. Chill for two hours, or till it turns stiff. Take fudge onto cutting board; remove wax paper. Slice into squares. Store loosely covered at room temperature. Prepares one to two pounds.

Chocolate Peppermint Drops

Ingredients

- 1 c. margarine, softened
- 2/3 c. dark brown sugar, packed
- 1 t. vanilla extract
- 2/3 c. sugar
- 1 t. peppermint extract
- 2 eggs, beaten
- 2 c. all-purpose flour
- 1 t. baking soda
- 1/2 t. salt
- 3/4 c. baking cocoa
- 1/2 c. candy canes, crushed

Directions

1. Mix margarine, sugars, extracts and eggs in a big bowl; mix properly. Put in rest of the ingredients excluding candy canes; Mix well. Chill for fifteen minutes, or until dough is easy to handle. Roll well-rounded teaspoons of dough into balls; set on parchment paper-lined baking sheets. Bake at three hundred twenty five degrees for twelve to thirteen minutes, or until cookies are puffed and centers are in place firmly. Take off of oven; with the back of a spoon, immediately and gently prepare a well in the center of cookies. Insert with a spoon about half teaspoon of crushed candy into well. Allow to stand for two to three minutes prior to removing from baking sheet. Prepares three and half dozen.

Minty Chocolate Cookie

Ingredients

- 18-1/2 oz. pkg. devil's food cake mix
- 1/2 c. oil
- 2 eggs, beaten
- 1 c. candy canes, crushed

Directions

1. Combine dry cake mix, eggs and oil; gently mix in crushed candy. Transfer by tablespoonfuls onto gently greased baking sheets. Bake at three hundred fifty degrees for about ten minutes; make sure not to overbake. Prepares three and half dozen.

Chocolate-Pecan Biscotti

Ingredients

- 1/2 c. butter, softened
- 1/4 c. baking cocoa
- 2 t. baking powder
- 2/3 c. powdered low-calorie sugar mix for baking
- 3 eggs, beaten
- 1-3/4 c. all-purpose flour
- 1/4 c. chopped pecans
- 1/2 c. sugar-free chocolate candy, chopped

Directions

1. Beat butter in a big bowl for thirty seconds. Put in sugar blend, cocoa and baking powder; beat till properly combined. Mix in eggs till properly mixed. Beat in as much flour as you can; Mix in rest of the flour by hand with wooden spoon. Mix in nuts and candy. Divide dough in half; roll into two, nine-inch long rolls. Make sure to arrange them on slightly greased baking sheets; flatten rolls to two inches wide. Bake at three hundred seventy five degrees for twenty to twenty five minutes; Make use of baking sheets for cooling for 1 hour. Place rolls on a cutting board; slice half-inch thick. Return slices sliced-side down to baking sheets; bake at three hundred twenty five degrees for eight minutes. Flip over and bake for an extra eight to nine minutes. Cool on a rack. Prepares about two and half dozen.

Chocolate-Peanut Butter Balls

Ingredients

- 1/2 c. butter
- 18-oz. jar creamy peanut butter
- 16-oz. pkg. powdered sugar
- 3-1/2 c. crispy rice cereal
- 18-oz. pkg. milk chocolate bar, chopped

Directions

1. Melt butter in a big saucepan over medium flame. Mix in peanut butter; Mix in powdered sugar and cereal. Prepare into 1-inch balls and set on wax paper. Melt chocolate on top of double boiler. Immerse balls in chocolate to coat; Make sure to arrange them on baking sheets to cool and firmly set. Prepares about five dozen.

Chocolate-Orange Snowballs

Ingredients

- 9-oz. pkg. vanilla wafers
- 1/4 c. baking cocoa
- 1/4 c. light corn syrup
- 2-1/4 c. powdered sugar, divided
- 1/3 c. frozen orange juice concentrate, thawed
- 1-1/2 c. chopped pecans

Directions

1. In a food processor, mix vanilla wafers, two cups powdered sugar, corn syrup, cocoa and orange juice concentrate. Process till the wafers are finely ground and mixture is well blended. Put in pecans and process till the nuts are properly chopped. Take mixture to a bowl; Prepare into 1-inch balls. Roll in rest of the powdered sugar. Keep in mind to store only in an airtight container. Prepares about five dozen.

Chocolotta Pizza

Ingredients

- 12-oz. pkg. semi-sweet chocolate chips
- 2 c. mini marshmallows
- 1 c. crispy rice cereal
- 8 2-oz. squares white melting chocolate, divided
- 6-oz. jar maraschino cherries, drained and halved
- 16-oz. pkg. candy-coated chocolate peanuts
- 1 t. oil

Directions

1. Mix chocolate chips and seven squares white chocolate in a two-quart microwave-safe bowl. Microwave over high setting for two minutes; stir. Microwave an extra one to two minutes, till it turns smooth, stirring every thirty seconds. Mix in marshmallows and cereal. Spoon onto a greased twelve inch pizza pan. Top with cherries and peanuts, pressing lightly. Microwave rest of the white chocolate with oil for 1 minute; stir. Microwave for thirty seconds to one minute, till it turns smooth, stirring every fifteen seconds. Sprinkle over pizza; chill till it turns stiff. Refrigerate until prepared to serve. Allow to stand at room temperature for ten to fifteen minutes prior to slicing into wedges. Prepares ten to twelve servings.

Brownie Pizza Slices

Ingredients

- 1 c. butter, divided
- 1-1/2 t. vanilla extract
- 3 eggs, beaten
- 1-1/2 c. sugar
- 3/4 c. baking cocoa, divided
- 1/2 t. baking powder
- 1/4 t. salt
- 3/4 c. all-purpose flour
- 1-1/2 c. powdered sugar
- 2 to 3 T. milk
- Garnish: mini chocolate chips, peanut butter candies, toasted coconut, toffee
- baking bits, chopped pecans

Directions

1. Melt three fourth cup butter; beat together with sugar, vanilla and eggs. Mix in half cup cocoa, flour,

baking powder and salt just until moistened. Spread into a greased nine inch pie plate. Bake at three hundred fifty degrees for sixteen to twenty minutes; make sure not to overbake. Test for completeness after sixteen minutes. Take off of oven; cool for ten minutes. Mix rest of the butter, powdered sugar, milk and rest of the cocoa. Spread over brownie in a thin, smooth layer. Using a sharp knife, cut brownie into eight wedges. Carefully remove each wedge and place on a wire rack. Drizzle gently wedges using a variety of garnishes, or leave as it is. Wrap each wedge in a plastic wrap or wax paper. Prepares eight servings.

Caramel Pecan Turtles

Ingredients

- 1 c. pecan halves
- 36 vanilla caramels
- 1/2 c. semi-sweet chocolate chips

Directions

1. Take a slightly oiled baking sheet, arrange five pecans together to prepare turtle legs and head. Place 1 caramel at the center of each turtle. Replicate with rest of the pecans and caramels. Bake at three hundred twenty five degrees for five to ten minutes, until caramels turn tender. Take off of oven and flatten caramel centers using a spatula. Melt chocolate chips in a saucepan over low flame; spoon over caramel centers. Cool till they are well set. Prepares about two and half dozen.

Creamy Chocolate Pecans

Ingredients

- 4 egg yolks
- 2/3 c. sugar
- 1-2/3 c. semi-sweet chocolate chips
- 2/3 c. whipping cream
- 1 t. vanilla extract
- 1/2 lb. pecan halves
- 14-oz. pkg. milk chocolate for melting

Directions

1. Beat egg yolks till they turn thick and attain a lemon color hue; Put in cream and sugar. Cook at the top of a double boiler over low flame until very thick. Place semi-sweet chocolate in a microwave bowl. Microwave over high setting for about one to two minutes, stirring every fifteen seconds; cool gently and put in to egg mixture. Mix in vanilla; beat properly and chill. Prepare into small balls; With a little force place a pecan half onto each side (two pecans per ball). Place milk chocolate in a microwave safe bowl. Microwave over high setting for one to two minutes, stirring every fifteen seconds until melted. Immerse balls into melted chocolate; Let cool on wax paper. Prepares about three dozen.

Chocolate Caramels

Ingredients

- 1-1/2 c. whipping cream

- 3/4 c. light corn syrup
- 3 1-oz. sqs. semi-sweet baking chocolate, chopped
- 1 c. sugar
- 1/4 t. salt

Directions

1. Mix all ingredients in a big saucepan over low flame. Cook, stirring continually, until mixture thickens and reaches the firm-ball stage, or two hundred forty five to two hundred fifty degrees on a candy thermometer. Pour into a gently buttered 8 inch x 4 inch loaf pan without scraping bottom of saucepan. Allow to stand till they are well set. Score candy into fifty squares using a knife. Place candy out onto a cool surface; turn over so scored side is facing up. Slice into squares along scored lines. Wrap each caramel in a piece of wax paper. Allow to stand in a cool place overnight; store at room temperature. Prepares about four dozen.

Espresso Bean Bark

Ingredients

- 12-oz. pkg. semi-sweet chocolate chips
- 1 t. margarine
- 3/4 c. whole coffee beans
- 1/4 c. white melting chocolate, chopped

Directions

1. Mix chocolate chips and margarine in a microwave-safe bowl. Microwave over high setting for two to three minutes, stirring every thirty seconds, until melted and smooth. Mix in coffee beans until uniformly distributed. Set onto a wax paper-lined baking sheet; spread uniformly. Drizzle gently with white chocolate; press gently. Freeze till they are well set, about five minutes. Crush into pieces; Keep in mind to store only in an airtight container. Prepares about twelve servings.

Tex-Mex Chocolate Snappers

Ingredients

- 1-3/4 c. all-purpose flour
- 1 t. cinnamon
- 1/4 t. salt
- 2 t. baking soda
- 1-1/2 c. sugar, divided
- 3/4 c. butter, softened
- 1 egg, beaten
- 1/4 c. light corn syrup
- 2 1-oz. envs. pre-melted unsweetened chocolate

Directions

1. Mix flour, baking soda, cinnamon and salt. Take a different bowl and beat together 1 cup sugar, butter and egg till it turns creamy. Put in corn syrup and pre-melted chocolate. Mix in flour mixture and shape into 1-inch balls. Roll balls in rest of the sugar to coat; set on ungreased baking sheets.

Bake for twelve to fifteen minutes. Prepares two dozen.

Coconut Bon-Bons

Ingredients

- 1/4 c. butter, softened
- 1 c. sweetened condensed milk
- 2 c. sweetened flaked coconut
- 16-oz. pkg. powdered sugar
- 9 1-oz. sqs. semi-sweet chocolate
- 2 T. shortening

Directions

1. Combine butter, powdered sugar and condensed milk. Mix in coconut. Roll into 1-inch balls; refrigerate till they are well set, about 1 hour. Melt chocolate and shortening in a double boiler over medium flame, stirring occasionally till it turns smooth. Take off of flame; stir till it is properly blended. Using a toothpick, Immerse balls into chocolate to coat. Place on wax paper to dry. Prepares about three dozen.

Cookies & Vanilla Cream Fudge

Ingredients

- 3 6-oz. pkgs. white chocolate chips
- 1/8 t. salt
- 14-oz. can sweetened condensed milk
- 2 c. chocolate sandwich cookies, coarsely crushed

Directions

1. Melt chocolate, condensed milk and salt in a big saucepan over low flame; stir till it turns smooth. Take off of flame; Mix in cookies. Spread uniformly in a greased aluminium foil-lined 8 inch x 8 inch baking pan. Let cool for two hours, or till it turns stiff. Take fudge onto cutting board; peel off foil and slice into squares. Keep in mind to store tightly covered at room temperature. Prepares about three and half dozen.

Mocha Pecan Fudge

Ingredients

- 1 c. chopped pecans
- fourteen-oz. can sweetened condensed milk
- 3 6-oz. pkgs. semi-sweet chocolate chips
- 2 T. strong brewed coffee, cooled
- 1 t. cinnamon
- 1/8 t. salt
- 1 t. vanilla extract

Directions

1. Place pecans in a microwave-safe pie plate. Microwave, uncovered, over high for four minutes,

stirring after each minute; place aside. In a large microwave safe bowl, mix chocolate chips, condensed milk, coffee, cinnamon and salt. Microwave, uncovered, over high setting for one to two minutes. Stir till it turns smooth. Mix in vanilla and pecans; immediately spread in a greased aluminium foil lined 8 inch x 8 inch baking pan. Cover and refrigerate till it turns stiff, about two hours. Take off of pan; cut into one-inch squares. Cover and store at room temperature. Prepares about five dozen.

Morgan's Crinkle Cookies

Ingredients

- 1/2 c. oil
- 1/4 c. butter
- 2 c. sugar
- 2 eggs
- 10 T. baking cocoa
- 1 t. vanilla extract
- 2 c. all-purpose flour
- 2 t. baking powder
- 1 t. salt
- 1 c. powdered sugar

Directions

1. Mix oil, butter, cocoa and sugar in a large bowl. Gently beat in eggs, one each time, till it is properly blended; Put in vanilla. Mix in flour, baking powder and salt. Let cool for two hours. Prepare into 1-inch balls and roll in powdered sugar. Make sure to arrange them on greased baking sheets. Bake at three hundred fifty degrees for eight to ten minutes. Prepares six to seven dozen.

Trillionaire Cookies

Ingredients

- 12-oz. jar caramel ice cream topping
- 36 round buttery crackers
- 1 c. pecans, finely chopped
- 12-oz. pkg. semi-sweet chocolate chips

Directions

1. Mix caramel topping and pecans in a saucepan over medium flame, stirring continually. Bring to a boil and cook for three to five minutes, until mixture thickens; Take off of flame. Place crackers on a wax paper-lined baking sheet. Drop about one to two teaspoons caramel mixture onto each cracker. Refrigerate for 1 hour, or till it turns stiff. In a small saucepan, melt chocolate over low flame, stirring continually. Take off of flame. With tongs, immerse each cracker in melted chocolate to reach the point of caramel filling; do not immerse filling. Return to baking sheet. Using a slotted spoon, sprinkle melted chocolate over cookies. Refrigerate for 1 hour, or until chocolate is set in place. Make sure to refrigerate only in an airtight container. Prepares three dozen.

Chocolate Truffle Cookies

Ingredients

- 1-1/4 c. butter, softened
- 1/3 c. baking cocoa
- 1/4 c. sour cream
- 2-1/4 c. powdered sugar
- 1 t. vanilla extract
- 2-1/4 c. all-purpose flour
- 12-oz. pkg. semi-sweet chocolate chips

Directions

1. Mix together butter, powdered sugar and cocoa. Mix in sour cream and vanilla; Put in flour and mix properly. Mix in chocolate chips. Allow to cool for 1 hour. Make dough into 1-inch balls; arrange two inches apart on ungreased baking sheets. Bake at three hundred twenty five degrees for fifteen minutes, or till they are well set. Cool for at least ten minutes on wire racks. Prepares two dozen.

Chocolate Bit Meringues

Ingredients

- 4 egg whites, at room temperature
- 1 t. vanilla extract
- 3 T. baking cocoa
- 1/2 t. cream of tartar
- 1 c. sugar
- 1 c. mini semi-sweet chocolate chips

Directions

1. Using an electric blender over high speed, beat egg whites in a big bowl until stiff. Put in cream of tartar and beat till they start to make stiff peaks. Put in vanilla, cocoa and sugar. Wrap in mini chocolate chips. Transfer by tablespoonfuls onto aluminium foil-lined baking sheets. Bake at two hundred fifty degrees for one hour and fifteen minutes, or till they are well set and dry. Allow to make use of baking sheets for cooling. Keep in mind to store only in an airtight container. Prepares three dozen.

Peanut Butter-Chocolate Fingers

Ingredients

- 1/2 c. margarine, softened
- 1/2 c. brown sugar, packed
- 1/2 c. sugar
- 1 egg, beaten
- 1/3 c. creamy peanut butter
- 1 c. quick-cooking oats, uncooked
- 1/2 t. baking soda
- 1/4 t. salt
- 1 c. all-purpose flour
- 1/2 t. vanilla extract

- 6-oz. pkg. semi-sweet chocolate chips

Directions

1. Mix margarine, sugars, egg and peanut butter; mix properly. Put in oats, flour, baking soda and salt; Mix in vanilla. Pour into a gently greased 13 inch x 9 inch baking pan. Bake at three hundred fifty degrees for twenty to twenty five minutes. Immediately drizzle gently with chocolate chips. Allow to stand until chocolate is melted; spread uniformly. Chill for ten to fifteen minutes, until chocolate is firm. Spread using frosting. Slice into rectangular "fingers." Prepares three dozen small bars or two dozen larger bars.

Frosting:

- 1/2 c. powdered sugar
- 1/4 c. peanut butter
- 2 to 4 t. milk

Mix all ingredients; mix till it turns smooth.

Double Fudgy Cookie Bars

Ingredients

- 24 chocolate sandwich cookies, divided
- 12-oz. pkg. semi-sweet chocolate chips, divided
- 14-oz. can sweetened condensed milk
- 1/4 c. butter, melted
- 1 t. vanilla extract

Directions

1. Place eighteen cookies in a food processor; process to coarse crumbs. Place aside rest of the cookies. Mix cookie crumbs and melted butter in a medium bowl till it is properly blended. Press into an ungreased 13 inch x11 inch baking pan; place aside. Mix 1 cup chocolate chips, condensed milk along with vanilla. Melt in a double boiler over medium flame, stirring frequently till it turns smooth. Spread chocolate mixture carefully over crumb crust; Drizzle gently with rest of the chocolate chips. Break rest of the cookies into pieces by hand; Drizzle gently over top. Bake at three hundred twenty five degrees for twenty to twenty five minutes. Refrigerate until chilled entirely; cut into bars. Prepares twenty.

North Pole Candy Cane Fudge

Ingredients

- 2 ten-oz. pkgs. white chocolate chips
- 1/2 t. peppermint extract
- 1-1/2 c. candy canes, crushed
- 14-oz. can sweetened condensed milk
- 1/8 t. red food coloring

Directions

1. Mix chocolate chips and condensed milk in a saucepan over low flame. Stir until nearly melted; Take off of flame and continue to stir till it turns smooth and entirely melted. Mix in extract, crushed candy and coloring. Spread uniformly in an aluminium foil-lined, greased 8 inch x 8 inch baking pan. Chill for two hours; cut into 1-inch squares. Prepares sixty five pieces.

Cool Mint Chocolate Swirls

Ingredients

- 3/4 c. butter
- 2 T. water
- 12-oz. pkg. semi-sweet chocolate chips
- 2 eggs
- 1-1/2 c. brown sugar, packed
- 2-1/2 c. all-purpose flour
- 1-1/4 t. baking soda
- 1/2 t. salt
- 3 4-1/2 oz. pkgs. crème de menthe wafer thins

Directions

1. In a saucepan over medium flame, mix butter, brown sugar and water. Cook, stirring in between, until melted. Take off of flame. Mix in chocolate chips until melted; cool for ten minutes. Pour chocolate mixture into a big bowl; Gently beat in eggs, one each time. Take a different bowl and mix flour, baking soda and salt; Mix in to chocolate mixture. Let cool dough for at least 1 hour. Shape into walnut-size balls; Make sure to place them two inches from each other on greased baking sheets. Bake at three hundred fifty degrees for eight to ten minutes; make sure not to overbake. With a little force place a mint wafer onto each cookie while still warm; Allow to stand for one minute. When mint softens, swirl mint over cookie using a spoon. Prepares three to four dozen.

Cocoa Buttercream Frosting

Ingredients

- 1/4 c. butter
- 3 T. baking cocoa
- 1 t. vanilla extract
- 2 c. powdered sugar
- 2 to 3 T. milk

Directions

1. Combine all ingredients excluding milk. Put in milk, a bit each time, until a smooth frosting consistency is attained. Prepares about 1 cup.

Homemade Hot Cocoa

Ingredients

- 1 c. milk
- 1/8 t. salt
- 2 T. baking cocoa

- 2 T. sugar

Directions

1. Mix ingredients in a small saucepan over medium-low flame. Cook and stir till it turns hot and bubbly. Take into a mug. Serves 1.

Nutty Butterscotch Crunch

Ingredients

- 12-oz. pkg. semi-sweet chocolate chips
- 2-1/2 c. dry-roasted peanuts
- 11-1/2 oz. pkg. butterscotch chips
- 4 c. chow mein noodles

Directions

1. Melt chocolate and butterscotch chips together at the top of a double boiler over partially seething water. Take off of flame; Put in peanuts. Mix in noodles till properly coated. Press into a buttered 13 inch x 9 inch baking pan. Chill till they are well set; slice into squares. Prepares two dozen.

Rocky Road Fudge

Ingredients

- 12-oz. pkg. semi-sweet chocolate chips
- 2 T. butter
- 14-oz. can sweetened condensed milk
- 3 c. dry-roasted peanuts
- ten-1/2 oz. pkg. mini marshmallows

Directions

1. Mix chocolate chips, condensed milk and butter in a saucepan over medium flame. Cook and mix till melts entirely. Take off of flame; Put in peanuts and marshmallows. Spread in a greased 13 inch x 9 inch baking pan. Chill till it turns stiff; cut into squares. Prepares three-four pounds.

Choco-Nut Dainties

Ingredients

- 1 c. margarine, softened and divided
- 1 egg, beaten
- 1-1/2 t. vanilla extract
- 3/4 c. sugar
- 2-1/4 c. all-purpose flour
- 6-oz. pkg. semi-sweet chocolate chips
- 1/2 t. salt
- 12-oz. pkg. semi-sweet chocolate chips
- Optional: 1 c. chopped walnuts

Directions

1. Beat together three fourths cup margarine, sugar, egg and vanilla in a big bowl till properly mixed. Put in flour and salt; Mix in smaller package of chocolate chips. On a gently floured surface, shape dough into two-inch by half-inch cylinders. Make sure to arrange them on ungreased baking sheets. Bake at three hundred fifty degrees for twelve to fifteen minutes; place placed on a wire rack to cool. Mix rest of the margarine and larger package of chocolate chips in a double boiler over medium flame. Mix till melts entirely and smooth; Take off of flame. Immerse ends of cookies into melted chocolate; roll in chopped nuts, if required. Place on wax paper till they are well set. Prepares about one and a half dozen.